THINKERS OF OUR TIME

SANTAYANA

by
Noël O'Sullivan

The Claridge Press
St Albans

All rights reserved. No part of this publication may be reproduced or transmitted in any form or by any means, including photocopying and recording, without the written permission of the copyright holder, application for which should be addressed to the Publishers. Such written permission must also be obtained before any part of this publication is stored in a retrieval system of any nature.

First published in Great Britain 1992

by The Claridge Press
27 Windridge Close
St Albans
Herts
AL3 4JP

Copyright © Noël O'Sullivan

Printed by
Short Run Press
Exeter, Devon

ISBN 1-870626-33-8 (Hardback)
ISBN 1-870626-38-9 (Paperback)

O'Sullivan, Noël: *Santayana*

1. Political Science
2. Philosophy

CONTENTS

Preface 5

Textual References 7

Introduction 9

Chapter 1: Life 13

Chapter 2: The Crisis of Western Humanism 23

Chapter 3: Towards a New Synthesis:
    the Philosophy of Naturalism 49

Chapter 4: Naturalism and Limited Politics 77

Chapter 5: Conclusion 103

Further Reading 107

Index 109

For
M.O'S

Preface

The aim of this book is to offer an overall interpretation of Santayana's diverse writings from a standpoint which has inevitably been obscured by studies that have concentrated on particular aspects of his work. Specifically, what will be suggested is that the unifying theme of his thought is the search for a philosophy of modesty appropriate to what it is now fashionable to call the post modern condition.

Santayana was an extraordinarily prolific writer whose exploration of this theme extended to every dimension of the human condition and was pursued in a variety of idioms, ranging from poetry and poetic drama, through literary criticism and a best-selling novel of his own, to philosophic essays and the construction of an ambitious philosophic system. I have tried to convey the breadth and flavour of his multi-faceted corpus, but have inevitably passed lightly over areas of his thought which, in a different context, would merit much more detailed attention. Nothing at all is said, for example, about his first philosophical work, on *Lotze's System of Philosophy,* and his important work on aesthetic is only touched upon obliquely. Whilst acknowledging the arbitrary element in what has been selected for emphasis, however, the theme chosen will be amply justified if it helps to awaken interest in Santayana's writings amongst those who have not yet discovered them, and to renew the interest of those who know them already.

I am grateful to Sebnem Gülfidan, Henning Heuerding, Rana Kurian, Gurpreet Mahajan, Archana Sharma, Jyotirmaya Sharma and Julia Stapleton for reading and commenting on various parts of the manuscript at different stages of composition. Stephen Kirby galvanized me into finishing it. Ranu Uniyal read and criticized the whole of the final version, as well as helping to prepare an index.

Bhikhu Parekh, David Norton and the late Robert Berki influenced my interpretation of many aspects of Santayana's work, in that intangible but all-pervasive way in which long-standing friendship influences every aspect of one's thought. With all three, agreement or disagreement was always an incidental matter, since they possessed the ultimate art of stopping one in one's tracks and making one think again.

The editor of the series, Roger Scruton, was at once patient, critical and encouraging and I am indebted to him on all three counts.

Textual references to Santayana's works

BR	Birth of Reason, New York 1968
CO	Character and Opinion in the United States, New York 1956
DL	Dialogues in Limbo, New York 1948
DP	Dominations and Powers, London 1951
E	Ethics, by Spinoza, Introduction by Santayana, London 1934
EGP	Egotism in German Philosophy, London 1916
FE	Five Essays: Some Turns of Thought in Modern Philosophy, Cambridge 1933
GT	The Genteel Tradition: Nine Essays by George Santayana, ed. D. L. Wilson, Cambridge, U.S.A. 1967
LE	Little Essays: Drawn from the Writings of George Santayana, London 1920
LGS	Letters of George Santayana, (ed. Daniel Cory), London 1955
LP	The Last Puritan, London 1935
LR	Life of Reason in five volumes, New York 1905 Vol 1, Reason in Common Sense; Vol 2, Reason in Society; Vol 3, Reason in Religion; Vol 4, Reason in Art; Vol 5, Reason in Science
MHW	My Host the World, (third volume of autobiography), London 1953
MS	The Middle Span, (second volume of autobiography), London 1947
OS	Obiter Scripta, London 1936
PGS	Philosophy of George Santayana, ed. P.A. Schilpp, Chicago 1940

P	Poems, New York 1923
PP	Persons and Places, (first volume of autobiography), London 1944
PR	Poetry and Religion, New York 1924
PSL	Platonism and the Spiritual Life, London 1927
RB	Realms of Being, (one vol. edition), New York 1942
SAF	Scepticism and Animal Faith, New York 1924
SB	The Sense of Beauty, New York 1896
SE	Soliloquies in England, London 1934
SCW	Selected Critical Writings, (2 vols.) ed. N. Henfrey, Cambridge 1968
TPP	Three Philosophical Poets, New York 1956
WD	Winds of Doctrine, London 1940

Introduction

Two rival interpretations of Santayana have prevailed since his death in 1952. According to the more favourable view, he is an elegant but elusive thinker, notable for his writings on select topics such as the nature of beauty or religion, but devoid of any overall theme of continuing relevance. According to the more hostile one, Santayana is a thinker who has simply ceased to speak to our age at all.

It would, of course, be foolish to suggest that this difference of opinion could ever be conclusively settled. It may plausibly be maintained, however, that Santayana not only saw clearly the main feature of our situation, but also offered a persuasive response to it which deserves more careful consideration than it has generally received.

What then is our situation? Santayana identifies it as the emergence of an industrial civilization, increasingly cut off from the classical and medieval roots which were, until recently, the source of western cultural life. This development has generally been regarded with dismay by other thinkers. Familiar expressions of despair include Max Weber's disenchanted vision of a coming spiritual ice-age; Heidegger's angst at the experience of finding himself flung into being; Sartre's somewhat similar nausea at his discovery that words and things do not necessarily coincide; and the incomprehensible intellectual debris of western humanism that flows from Lucky in Beckett's *Waiting for Godot*.

Santayana's response to the disintegration of our cultural tradition, by contrast, is altogether more positive and constructive. It is this which distinguishes him from the majority of twentieth century thinkers.

Although his standpoint is profoundly sceptical, his scepticism is never merely iconoclastic. Above all, he has no doubt that men may still achieve what Spinoza, the philosopher whom he admired most in the modern world, defined as the supreme good: 'the knowledge', that is, 'of the union which the mind has with the whole of nature' (E 230). He believes, moreover, that this knowledge can be achieved without any of the existential posing, or irrational leaps into faith, which have been proposed by other philosophers. What then is the nature of the philosophy which enables Santayana to avoid the gloomy conclusion that the modern world moves only ever deeper into the wasteland?

Philosophy, as Santayana understands it, has two dimensions. On the one hand, there is the formal dimension, in which it is narrowly conceived of as an investigation into truth. The fact that Santayana considers this dimension unduly narrow does not mean that he feels it can be treated casually: on the contrary, his major works are rigorous attempts to deal with the logical, metaphysical and epistemological problems that this formal dimension of philosophy entails. There is, however, a second dimension, distinct from the formal one and more fundamental than it, since without it the formal, analytic dimension would lack any significant purpose.

The core of this second dimension is vision. In this dimension, philosophy is linked with poetry. In Santayana's own words, the substance of the philosophic vision 'is sublime. The order it reveals in the world is something beautiful, tragic, sympathetic to the mind or just what every poet, on a small or on a large scale, is always trying to catch' (TPP 17). In the last resort, the formal side of philosophy is only a means to the achievement of this vision, which is 'insight':

> In philosophy itself investigation and reasoning are only the preparatory and servile parts, means to an end. They terminate in insight or what in the noblest sense of the word may be called *theory*, Oewpia, — a steady contemplation of all things in their order and worth. Such contemplation is imaginative. No one can reach it who has not enlarged his mind and trained his heart. A philosopher who attains it is, for the moment, a poet; and a poet who turns his practised and passionate imagination on the order of all things, or on anything in the light of the whole, is for that moment a philosopher (TPP 17-18).

It is this dimension of Santayana's philosophy — that is, the overall vision which inspires it — with which the present book is especially concerned. The term vision, it should perhaps be added, is not intended to connote some kind of mysticism. What it involves is best described by Nietzsche's phrase, a transvaluation of values, since Santayana's goal is simply the reformulation of familiar problems from a standpoint that has been purged of the unconscious egotism and anthropocentrism which permeate traditional philosophy.

In Santayana's case, however, the outcome of this transvaluation is far closer to Montaigne's sober attitude than to Nietzsche's extravagant cult of the *Ubermensch*. Indeed, Santayana notes, his own vision is the same as the one Montaigne described when he wrote:

> He who sets before him, as in a picture, this vast image of our mother Nature in her entire majesty; who reads in her aspect such universal and continual variety; who discerns himself therein and not himself only but a whole kingdom, to be but a most delicate dot — he alone esteems things according to the just measure of their greatness (Quoted in EGP 165).

It is against the background of this vision that Santayana undertook, in *Dominations and Powers*, one of the most ambitious attempts to restate the intellectual foundations of the western ideal of limited politics that the twentieth century has witnessed. Although it is, as we shall see, a flawed attempt, it remains of continuing interest at a time when the framework of discussion has increasingly become confined to a debate between defenders of the free market, on the one hand, and advocates of collectivist planning, on the other. Within that framework it has been possible to discuss such topics as social justice, public choice theory, and the nature of rights; but the first principles of limited politics remain concealed from sight. It is to Santayana's credit that *Dominations and Powers* re-opens consideration of those principles.

Before considering his political thought, however, it will be useful to begin with a short account of Santayana's life, with the development of his philosophy in mind. This will be followed, in the second chapter, by an examination of the radical critique he launches against practically the whole of the western intellectual tradition since the time of Socrates. In chapter three, the alternative basis upon which he sought to re-establish the tradition will be explored. Against this background we may return, in chapter four, to his politics.

Chapter 1: Life

The salient facts of George Santayana's life are soon told. He was born in Madrid in 1863. His parents were middle class, although his father's side of the family treasured an unconfirmed claim to noble lineage. When he was three, his mother returned to the U.S.A. to bring up the children of her first marriage to an American husband, who had died in 1857. Santayana remained in Spain with his father until 1872, when he was taken to join his mother in Boston. After distinguishing himself first at school and then at Harvard College, from which he graduated in 1886, he was appointed to the Harvard philosophy department in 1889. In 1912 he suddenly gave up his professorship. Possessing private means, he was able to live and travel at leisure in Europe. He eventually took up residence at an hotel in Rome in 1924. Italy became his home from that time until his death. He remained there during the Second World War, taking rooms in 1941 in the Convent of the Blue Nuns, where he died in 1952. He never married, remarking in his autobiography that 'I am a born cleric, or poet' (PP 166).

The unifying thread which runs through Santayana's life and thought is the experience of solitude. This was not, he emphasized, a source of misery to him, like the sense of loneliness and alienation which has afflicted many of the intellectuals of our century, but a preferred condition. The 'sense of belonging elsewhere, or rather of not belonging where I lived', he remarked, 'was nothing anomalous or unpleasant to me but, as it were, hereditary. My father had done his life-work in a remote colony; my mother had no home as a child, her first husband had been of one nationality and her second husband of another, and she had always been a stranger, like me, wherever she was. This', he noted, 'is rather consonant with my philosophy and may have helped to form it' (PGS 602).

Until his middle years there was relatively little outward indication of Santayana's inner sense of solitude. He was sociable and, during his early years at least, made close friends not only at Harvard, but at Oxford and Cambridge as well. Notable amongst these were C.A. Strong, at Harvard, and Bertrand Russell's brother, the second Earl Russell, at Cambridge.

Santayana's sense of solitude seemed no more to impair the steady progress of a brilliant academic and literary career than it impaired his sociability. In particular, his first philosophical work *The Sense of Beauty* (1896), and the five volumes of *The Life of Reason* (1905-6) which followed it a decade later, gained him widespread professional respect. The considerable reputation which he had acquired by the time of the First World War is testified to by the fact, for example, that Bertrand Russell was glad to acknowledge that Santayana's criticism (in *Winds of Doctrine*, 1913) of his ethical philosophy had led him to abandon moral absolutism in favour of the relativism fundamental to Santayana's own philosophical position. Another eminent thinker who subsequently acknowledged the durable influence of pre-war encounter with Santayana was T.S. Eliot, one of Santayana's students at Harvard, who expressed indebtedness to *Three Philosophical Poetss* (1910) in particular. The general opinion of their teacher held by Santayana's more able students may be gleaned from a 1912 edition of *The Harvard Monthly* which records that he had 'attained at Harvard a following which in enthusiasm and intensity, if not in numbers (was) almost impossible to parallel,' adding that students were aware of 'greatness in his presence,' and of 'completeness and grandeur' (SCW 1,4).

Outward reality, however, was one thing, and the inner world another. Although Santayana accepted his parents' amicable decision to live in two different countries, the childhood move to the United States intensified a sense of spiritual disorientation for which social and professional success provided no adequate remedy. Nevertheless, he fully acknowledged the advantages of the upbringing he received in the U.S., and paid generous tribute to the qualities of American character, foremost amongst which was 'a fund of vigour, goodness, and hope such as no nation ever possessed before. In what sometimes looks like American greediness and jostling for the first place,' he added, 'all is love of achievement and nothing is unkindness; it is a fearless people, and free from malice' (CO vi). His experience of life in the U.S.A. became the subject of two critical but sympathetic analyses of American culture which remain instructive, viz. an essay on *The Genteel Tradition in American Philosophy* (1911) and *Character and Opinion in the United States* (1920).

As Santayana's response to America indicated, his Spanish identity remained the core of his being. His childhood departure from the old world, he observed, had meant 'a terrible moral disinheritance'. Despite his tributes to the new world, he encountered beneath all the good qualities there 'an emotional and intellectual chill, a pettiness and practicality of outlook and ambition, which I should not have encountered amid the complex passions and intrigues of a Spanish environment...' (PP 15).

Santayana recalled in his autobiography how, from 1883 to 1930, he found partial relief from this sense of spiritual dislocation in what he described as an annual pilgrimage to Spain. He always went to Avila, a small and ancient town to which his parents had moved when he was three. Until he was seventy, Avila remained 'the centre of my deepest legal and affectionate ties...(and) gave me a most firm and distinctive station' (PP 103). There, where modernization had not yet created mental confusion and moral anarchy, everything involved a sense of continuity with an ancient past: 'the walls, the streets, the churches, the language, still bore witness to a faded but abiding civilization' (PP 117). Life there was sad, he observed; but it was also more natural than in modern societies. People, he noted, 'were simply resigned to the realities of mother nature and of human nature; and in its simplicity their existence was deeply civilized, not by modern conveniences but by moral tradition' (PP 117).

Santayana missed, in particular, the exuberant joy of the Spanish carnival. He also missed Catholicism, the religion in which he had grown up. What oppressed him most about America was the all-pervasiveness of Calvinist moralism, with its religion of duty and material success. Although he was never a practising Catholic, and never subscribed to any dogma, he loved the mythical and poetical side of Catholicism, finding in it a body of symbols which accurately portrayed man's relation to the world, rather than a literal description of the nature of the universe. It was this view of religion which he developed in an early work on *Poetry and Religion* (1900), where he argued that ' religion and poetry are identical, in essence, and differ merely in the way in which they are attached to practical affairs' (PR 8).

Santayana's concern with the relation between religion and poetry, it may be noticed, echoes the late nineteenth century cultural climate in which his formative years were spent. That climate was marked by a mixture of idealism, romanticism, and positivism, of which various permutations were frequently used by contemporaries to make good the spiritual void created by the decline of religious faith. Looking back on this era in middle years, Santayana reminded a friend that 'we were not very much later than Ruskin, Pater, Swinburne, and Matthew Arnold: our atmosphere was that of poets and parsons touched with religious enthusiasm or religious sadness...' (SCW 1,16). Although his sympathy for religion was accompanied by an equally fundamental love of beauty, he was always too robust by temperament, as well as too philosophically rigorous, to succumb to the aestheticism to which his contemporaries were prone.

Santayana restated the same view of religion he had developed in 1900 towards the end of his life, in *The Idea of Christ in the Gospels, or God in Man* (1946). It is a view of religion which is easily ridiculed, as indeed it had been earlier by the wit who remarked that Santayana believed there is no God and that Mary is His mother. A more sympathetic view would note, instead, Santayana's regard for the synthesis of experience achieved by St. Thomas Aquinas, and would find that his paradoxes soon dissolved, when interpreted in the light of the distinction between essence and existence which he shared with the Scholastic tradition, and which became the basis of his own philosophy.

Sympathy for the Catholic religion and the disappearing world to which it belonged did not, it should be stressed, lead Santayana into a reactionary rejection of modernity. Quite the contrary, whilst acknowledging that Avila provided a welcome refuge, he attached no less importance to the life of New England, which he described as the second centre of his existence. In fact, he observed, 'The extreme contrast between the two centres and the two influences became itself a blessing: it rendered flagrant the limitations and the contingency of both' (PP 103). Above all, no place could have been friendlier than Harvard. In the end, however, he could not come to terms with Harvard, where 'a wealth of books and much generous intellectual sincerity went with such spiritual penury and moral confusion as to offer nothing but a lottery ticket or a chance at the grab-bag to the orphan mind' (PP 104). No matter how brilliant the figures whom he met and studied with there — figures like Royce and William James — the intellectual world they occupied was not 'vital'. Their culture was either a 'genteel tradition', floating on the surface of a society with which it had no organic connection, or a dogmatic pragmatism. In either case, its core was moralism. This, it will be seen later, was to be one of the central targets of Santayana's attack on the western intellectual tradition.

The latent conflict between Santayana's inner and outer life finally surfaced in 1912. To the surprise of his friends and acquaintances, he not only resigned his post at Harvard and left America for good, but also abandoned professional academic life at large. What had repelled him from the start, he explained in his autobiography, was the idea of being a 'professional' at all; the fact that he seemed good at it was irrelevant. 'What I wanted', he wrote, 'was to go on being a student, especially to be a travelling student....I could have made a bargain with Mephistopheles, not for youth but for the appearance of youth, so that with its tastes but without its passions, I might have been a wandering student all my life' (PP 258).

Santayana spent the war years in England, to which he had been deeply attached ever since his first visit in 1886, shortly after graduating. He found there, he wrote, a *tertium quid* between the moral superficiality of the New World, on the one hand, and the 'cocky' and 'effusive' Latins of the old world, on the other. His reservations about Latins were accompanied by similar ones about Teutons, especially 'the dense vanity and officiousness' of the Germans, 'that nothing can put to shame' (SE 3-4).

What attracted him, he admitted, was largely the England of his own imagination — an idealized England, that is, in which he found the 'contentment in finitude, fair outward ways, [the] manly perfection and simplicity' he also associated with ancient Greece (SE 2). Despite the idealized character of his England, his love for the country was real: 'no climate, no manners, no companions on earth could be more congenial to my complexion' (SE 4). The English language, moreover, was the only one he ever claimed to be able to speak with any assurance. His proficiency was such, indeed, that he published several volumes of poetry in English. As he explained in one of these volumes, however, even his proficient grasp of the language did not modify the ultimate sense of being a stranger. 'Its roots', he observed of the English language, 'do not quite reach my centre' (P viii).

Since there was no question of finding in England the spiritual harmony he now sought with increasing intensity, he turned down the invitation of a fellowship at Oxford and eventually moved, after the war, to Italy. He could look back, since leaving America, on a productive decade. Especially notable was the publication, in 1916, of *Egotism in German Philosophy*. Although widely taken for one of the spate of anti-German war books, the themes it presented had long been with Santayana and were not, as some commentators complacently assumed, peculiar to the German intellectual tradition. *Soliloquies in England* (1922) was a further fruit of the same period. Taken in conjunction with a third volume, *Character and Opinion in the United States* (1920), he wrote, these volumes marked 'my emancipation from official control and professional pretensions'. Henceforth, 'all was now a voluntary study,' in which 'the point of view had become at once frankly personal and speculatively transcendental. A spirit, the spirit in a stray individual, was settling its accounts with the universe. My official career had happily come to an end' (MS 191).

After moving to Rome, Santayana noted, his physical orbit became constantly narrower (MHW 73). His intellectual life, likewise, became increasingly concentrated upon the detached contemplation of eternal essences. Whether this is to be regarded as a deepening of his ideal of spirituality, or merely an escape from the world into a rarefied intellectualism, is a matter for subsequent discussion. The philosophic landmarks in this process of withdrawal are *Scepticism and Animal Faith* (1923), which contained the outline of Santayana's mature system; *Platonism and the Spiritual Life* (1927); and *Realms of Being* (1928-40), his *magnum opus*. *Dialogues in Limbo* (1926) presented the central themes of the mature philosophy in an accessible, but still demanding, literary form; whilst what he called a 'philosophic novel', *The Last Puritan* (1935), explored their emotional implications so successfully that it became a best-seller, rapidly translated into German and Swedish.

Santayana remained in Rome during the Second World War. A late letter to an American correspondent described his attitude to Fascism:

> Of course I was never a Fascist in the sense of belonging to that Italian party, or to any nationalistic or religious *party*. But considered, as it is for a naturalist, a product of the generative order of society, a nationalist or religious *institution* will probably have its good sides, and be better perhaps than the alternative that presents itself at some moment in some place. That is what I thought, and still think, Mussolini's dictatorship was for Italy in its home government. Compare it with the disorderly socialism that preceded or the impotent party chaos that has followed it. If you had lived through it from beginning to end, as I have, you would admit this. But Mussolini personally was a bad man and Italy a half-baked political unit; and the *militant* foreign policy adopted by Fascism was ruinous in its artificiality and folly. But internally, Italy was, until the foreign militancy and mad alliances were adopted, a stronger, happier, and more united country than it is or had ever been. Dictatorships are surgical operations, but some diseases require them, only the surgeon must be an expert, not an adventurer' (LGS 405, italics in the original).

Although Santayana defended his attitude towards Fascism in the manner indicated, it is important to add that he regarded the topic as of only incidental significance from the broader standpoint of philosophy. In that perspective, he insisted, 'it is what people intend or actually do that interests me, not what they think they or others ought to do' (LGS 438). It is a position which many have found hard to accept, but his last work, *Dominations and Powers* (1951), is consistent with his naturalism in assigning to political philosophy a purely descriptive role. Although that work is profoundly critical of liberalism, it reveals an equally deep personal commitment to pluralism and limited government.

Santayana died not long after the publication of *Dominations and Powers*. There are two conflicting accounts of his death, of which details are given in Father Richard Butler's *The Life and Work of George Santayana* (1960). One account, which is ascribed to the nun (Sister Angela) who attended to him during the last ten years of his life and was with him till the end, runs as follows. Immediately before the final coma, he recovered consciousness briefly and was asked by Sister Angela whether he was suffering. He replied that he was no longer suffering physically, but mentally. When the nun asked what the matter was, he uttered one word in anguish: 'Desperation!' He never spoke again.

The alternative account is given by Santayana's friend and secretarial assistant, Daniel Cory. Cory describes long and complicated philosophical conversations, in the Socratic manner. In these conversations, Santayana adhered unwaveringly to his naturalistic system, and insisted near the end: 'My anguish is physical, there are no moral difficulties whatsoever'.

Father Richard, who knew the nun, attempted to check the facts with her once more, after the publication of Cory's account. By then, she too had died.

As this short account of his life will have indicated, Santayana was not the kind of thinker to found a school of philosophy, or even to want to influence anyone at all. The concluding words of his *Apologia Pro Mente Sua* (1940), in which he replied to some of his leading contemporary critics, convey the sentiments he wished to transmit to those who, living after him, might show some interest in his work.

Since they are sentiments worthy of a philosopher, and ones which do as much justice to Santayana's characteristic eloquence as to his intellectual modesty, they provide an apt ending to this chapter:

> If by chance a group of persons anywhere were brought to accept my philosophy, I am sure this would be done at the cost of misrepresenting it; I mean, by not understanding it as I do, but giving it some other twist, perhaps nearer to the truth of the matter... It is honour enough to be read and studied, even if only to be combated; and I send my critics back to their respective camps with my blessing, hoping that the world may prove staunch and beautiful to them, pictured in their own terms (PGS 605).

Chapter 2: The Crisis of Western Humanism

For Santayana, the principal feature of contemporary western civilization is the final disintegration of the humanist tradition which has hitherto provided the basis of our moral, political and religious beliefs. The result is a situation of complete cultural dislocation in which 'the modern world has missed its way' (BR 49). Accordingly, the principal task of contemporary intellectual life is to mitigate the spiritual chaos at the heart of our civilization by a radical restatement of the humanist tradition. Unless this is done, we shall rapidly pass from civilization to barbarism, since there will no longer be any means of identifying the limits upon which all civilization depends. To connect the humanist tradition with a rational theory of limits is thus the central concern of Santayana's philosophy, which offers one of the most profound and subtle responses to the crisis of humanism that the present century has witnessed. In order to understand this response it is necessary to begin by looking more closely at why the crisis has occurred and what it involves.

So far as the origins of the crisis are concerned, Santayana is emphatic that they are not to be found in any of the directions in which they are usually sought, such as the rise of capitalism, the worship of science, or the decline of Christianity (MHW 176). The main origin is at once simpler and more deep-seated, consisting in the fact that 'The contemporary world has turned its back on the attempt and even on the desire to live reasonably' (MHW 179). It has done so, not from caprice, but from folly. More precisely, the folly of modernity is to have surrendered to a naive dream. According to this dream, the growth of science and extensive social and political reform can between them make all mankind rich, free and happy. The dream is in fact a delusion. It is a delusion, because it lacks altogether the essential trait of rational living, which is to have 'a clear, sanctioned, ultimate aim'. In place of such an aim there is only the cry for 'vacant freedom and indeterminate progress', without any contemplation of the possibility that this cry might serve only to point modernity towards 'a bottomless pit' (MHW 182).

Our need, then, is for a revision of humanism which will restore the conditions for rational living. These, Santayana writes, may be reduced to two: 'First, self-knowledge, the Socratic key to wisdom; and second, sufficient knowledge of the world to perceive what alternatives are open to you and which of them are favourable to your true interests' (MHW 179). The immediate task is to examine more closely what Santayana considered to be the main obstacle to rational living. Although the obvious enemy is the dream of emancipation just mentioned, this is only the tip of an iceberg beneath which, Santayana wrote, 'the elements in [the] crisis have been lurking in the body-politic for ages, ever since the Reformation, not to say since the age of the Greek Sophists and of Socrates' (MHW 184). The concealed part of the iceberg consists of three deep-rooted sources of closure of experience, each of which alienates man from himself and from the world. They may be identified as realism, moralism and rationalism.

Realism

Realism is the belief that all true knowledge involves the description of an external reality. This is the assumption which unites the three great intellectual systems which have thus far dominated the western tradition, viz. the metaphysics of the ancient world, the theology of the medieval world, and the scientific vision of the modern world. In each case, reality is approached from an empirical, or quasi-empirical, standpoint which identifies true knowledge with the quest for the accurate description of an external object. This object may, of course, be conceived of in entirely different ways. In Plato's case, for example, it consists of the eternal forms contemplated by the philosopher; in the medieval world, the external object was God; and in the modern world the object is the empirical facts which are assumed to be revealed by the experimental method of natural science.

In every case, what is never explicitly acknowledged by these realist approaches is the part played by human imagination in constructing the world in which man lives. In consequence, the imaginative symbolism which clothes the world we encounter is systematically misunderstood as a more or less confused and unsatisfactory attempt to describe material facts.

The inevitable result of this misunderstanding has been a recurrent tendency of the western tradition to reject as worthless the only kind of symbolism which can give meaning to life. It was this confusion, for example, which led the Sophists to undermine the myths of the ancient world. In the modern world, the nature of religion has been misunderstood as the result of a similar confusion. Like myth, what religion actually offers is poetic or figurative truth; it portrays, that is, an ideal reality, not an empirical world. In the modern period, however, both myth and religion have for long been dismissed as childish substitutes for scientific truth, because they have generally been regarded as more or less crude attempts to portray an external world (LE 79-80). In this respect, Santayana observes, religion has frequently been to blame for the confusion about its nature, since it has not always resisted the temptation to claim that it is attempting to describe the facts of material existence. When this happens, it not only impoverishes its own distinctive ideal vision of life, but also lapses into a foolish and fanatical competition with natural science.

Perhaps the best way of understanding the disastrous practical consequences of realism, however, as well as the nature of the philosophical error it involves, is to reflect upon a story which graphically conveys Santayana's vision of life. Once upon a time, so the story runs, the whole world was a garden, over which there presided an old woman, who was really a goddess in disguise. The old woman lived in a cave, and only came out at night. In her hand she carried a long-handled pruning-hook, and with it she silently pruned everything in the garden: no tree or shrub escaped, and in addition she frequently trimmed the flowers and plants as well.

Now in this beautiful garden there lived a child, Autologos, who played there alone. In his play, the child gave names to everything that he liked or disliked, and in particular to the flowers and plants that interested him. The rose, for example, he called Beauty, the thistle Pain, and the violet Sadness. What Santayana stresses is that these flowers and plants were so beautiful and important to the child that he assumed that the names he gave them stood for qualities intrinsic to the nature of the flowers and plants themselves. One day, however, the child pricked himself with the thorns of a rose, and in consequence decided to change her name from Beauty to Love. This was a fateful decision, because it caused the child to wonder why he had given these particular names to everything rather than quite different names. As he reflected, he suddenly felt disenchanted with the garden, for what he had taken to be a world of absolute values, quite independent of himself, now seemed to collapse into purely subjective projections of his own concerns on to the plants and flowers. Alas, the child now ceased to play, and abandoned himself instead to his sorrowful thoughts.

Whilst he was brooding, a man in a black gown came into the garden. He was a botanist, proud of his scientific way of looking at things. The botanist explained to the child that the true names of flowers are scientific names, and that to call a rose Beauty or Love is not really to describe it at all, but to indulge one's fancy. Then the child grew even sadder, and the botanist tried to comfort him by saying that there was no harm in calling the flowers by whatever names the child chose. But the child was in despair, and would not be comforted. With a mixture of anguish and anger, he turned to the botanist and said: 'If I cannot give beautiful names to the plants and flowers which shall be really their souls, and if I cannot tell myself true tales about them, I will not play in the garden any more. You may have it all to yourself and botanize in it, but I hate you'. And then the child went to sleep.

During the night, the old woman came with her pruning-knife and cut off the child's head. The next morning the botanist returned and was filled with misery when he could not find the child. Being a scientist, the botanist was indifferent to the beauty of the flowers. The botanist died almost immediately, having become aware of the futility of a profession which was wholly utilitarian in outlook.

In this story, the goddess symbolizes the indifferent order of the universe, which goes its way neither with any special sympathy for man's dreams, nor with any particular hostility to them. The child symbolizes the power of imagination to endow the human world with meaning and significance. The child also symbolizes the folly of those who create for themselves a spurious sense of alienation, nausea, and despair by dismissing the work of imagination as pure illusion, simply because it does not provide a literal description of the facts of nature. The fate of the botanist drives the message home, symbolizing as it does the folly of those who impoverish reality by dismissing the world of value as purely subjective.

If we now drop the symbolism, the philosophical point of the story is clear: it is that no new synthesis of experience is possible if the realist quest for literal meaning continues to discredit the central place of imagination, and the symbolic forms which express it, in human existence. Until the imagination has time 'to recover and to reassert its legitimate and kindly power', Santayana writes, 'the European races [will] be reduced to confessing that while they have mastered the mechanical forces of nature, both by science and by the arts, [they] have become incapable of mastering or understanding themselves, and that, bewildered like the beasts by revolutions of the heavens and by their own irrational passions, they [can] find no way of uttering the *ideal* meaning of their life' (LE 80).

This critique of realism links Santayana to philosophers, such as Nietzsche, who have emphasized the crucial importance of myth as the ultimate source of meaning and significance in life. In Nietzsche, however, the idea of myth tends to suggest flight into a purely subjective world, in which the imaginative has been equated with the imaginary. For Santayana, by contrast, to understand the nature of imaginative symbolism properly is the key to restoring objectivity to the world of moral, political and aesthetic values. This is impossible, however, so long as a deeply established prejudice about the nature of objectivity continues to inspire western thought about values. According to that prejudice, which is the core of the realist attitude, objectivity only exists when values are disconnected from human emotions.

Realist philosophers, Santayana observes, 'seem to feel that unless moral and aesthetic judgments are expressions of objective truth, and not merely expressions of human nature, they stand condemned of hopeless triviality. A judgment is not trivial, however, because it rests on human feeling; on the contrary, triviality consists in abstraction from human interests, of which the knowledge of truth is one, but one only' (LE 3). It follows that the elimination of the alienation produced by realism involves more than abstract intellectual argument; what it requires is the elimination of the almost pathological contempt for the emotional seat of human-nature. Without this change of attitude, it is impossible to counter the potentially nihilistic prejudice which western man has often seemed to entertain against himself. It is this prejudice which finds philosophic expression in the realist conviction that 'anything which is a product of [man's] mind seems to him to be unreal and comparatively insignificant. We are satisfied only when we fancy ourselves surrounded by objects and laws independent of our nature' (LE 3).

It was the glory of pre-Socratic philosophy, Santayana believes, to have succeeded in retaining the openness to imaginative experience which was subsequently destroyed by realism. Prior to Socrates, Greek philosophers had clearly distinguished between the study of nature, which is the object of scientific inquiry, and the study of the products of self-consciousness, with which moral and psychological inquiry is concerned. The early philosophers had treated both types of inquiry as equally valid, refusing to engage in the kind of arbitrary privileging of one type of experience at the expense of the other which has subsequently bedeviled the western intellectual tradition (BR 147).

The main difficulty created by Santayana's search for a theory of imaginative symbolism with which to replace the distortions of a destructive realism is obvious: he was constantly threatened by the danger of falling into a subjectivism as extreme as that which he criticised. This danger is clear, for example, when he recommends that we should learn our philosophy from the other animals in the world, since it is unlikely that they are as readily deceived as we are by the senses:

> When they notice the sky, for instance, they surely never say to themselves that it is round, or even that it is blue or cloudy or starry. In each case they take the sensation for a vital stimulus as they would heat or cold, not for an independent object. Independent objects are wisely limited to things that arouse fear, attraction or hatred, or that are actually being devoured or seized. Animals therefore take such imagination as they may have for what it really is, a vain dream, or a useful sign, but never for a revelation of intangible realities (BR 139).

The problem about learning philosophy from animals is, of course, that they have no need for it, being unaware of any distinction between the real and the imaginary, or the subjective and the objective. Further consideration of Santayana's attempt to escape from a purely subjective theory of imagination must, however, be postponed for the moment.

Moralism

If the closure of experience effected by realism impoverishes and destabilizes the humanist tradition by its implicit contempt for imagination and emotion, the closure brought about by moralism results in an even deeper kind of alienation from life. Moralism is the equation of the real with the good. It occurs, that is, when the moral perspective is elevated into an absolute one. This is the great vice of both the classical and the Christian traditions of western culture. In its classical form, moralism first emerged with the philosophies of Plato and Aristotle. It is the philosophy of Plato, however, which reveals the destructive implications of moralism most clearly.

In Plato's case, Santayana maintains, moralism consisted in the elevation of Greek political consciousness into an ontological principle. The hinge of Plato's moralism, to be precise, was his conviction that the universe itself 'could never be anything but a crystal case to hold the jewel of a Greek city' (PGS 547). The constricting effect of this moralism is manifest in Plato's intolerant attitude to the infinite diversity of human nature. This intolerance is reflected, for example, in the fact that Plato's philosophers 'were *Guardians*, not poets, lovers, or free philosophers'. Moralism is the explanation, more generally, for the arbitrary restriction of any prospect of realizing the ideal good to 'a few desiccated doctrinaires entrenched in a tower. The young and the inspired might have realized their perfection also; it would not have been denied to women and children and slaves: they might all have touched it, I mean, in passing, which is all that the wisest soul can ever do, or the happiest city' (PGS 549). Moralism is reflected, likewise, in the draconian legislation against impiety in the *Laws*, where measures are advocated to ensure that gods not conscripted in the service of the city-state would be banished both from the universe and from the human heart (PGS 548).

Had Plato been more sensitive to the variety inherent in nature, 'he might have retained in his ideal more of what had rendered those many cities so beautiful in their youth: the spontaneous spirituality of intuition (which he certainly loved) and the measured impression of all the passions' (PGS 548). It is obvious from these remarks that, although Santayana was hostile to liberalism, a profound tolerance for diversity was a natural consequence of his rejection of the closure of experience brought about by moralism.

Moralism is not restricted to Plato: Aristotle too is guilty of this error. In his case, it assumes the form of the pseudo-science of metaphysics, which is at bottom nothing more than 'humanism materialised' (PGS 519). When Aristotle added first philosophy or theology — those being his own descriptions of metaphysics — to his natural philosophy or physics, he was under the impression that he was merely continuing his physics at a deeper level. In reality,

Santayana maintains, he was introducing postulates and presuppositions which have no place in natural philosophy. Specifically, what Aristotle did was to introduce the Socratic assertion that the good is the secret of the real: 'This good was partly moral, the self-sufficing, perfect, or blessed, and partly intellectual, the clear, the definite, the eternal'. The result was that physics 'was not backed by a moral and logical reason for the facts that it described: it had become metaphysics' (PGS 519).

The ultimate delusion fostered by moralism, then, is the belief that there is a reason or ground for man's existence. Moralism, that is, is the source of what is now called a 'foundational' approach to philosophy. In fact, 'existence is groundless, essentially groundless; for if I thought I saw a ground for it, I should have to look for a ground for that ground, *ad infinitum*. I must stop at the *quia*, the brute fact' (PGS 505). There is more than logic at stake here, however, since the philosophical search for a reason for existence has a powerful emotional basis. This search, Santayana maintains, is nothing less than a kind of madness, consisting of an impossible desire to eliminate the inescapable contingency of all existence.

By concealing the ultimate contingency of being, moralism obviously performs a seemingly attractive function for human life — it offers the consolation of a meaningful world. This consolation is bought, however, at the expense of the dignity which comes from facing the truth. In this respect Santayana's sentiments are those of the Stranger who, in one of his imaginary dialogues with Socrates, embraces the absurdity of existence with positive relish. 'Nothing can reconcile me to my personality', the Stranger observes, 'save the knowledge that it is an absurd accident, that things pleasanter to think of exist in plenty, and that I may always retire from it into pure spirit with its impartial smile' (DL 154). What Santayana means by spirit will be explored later; for the moment it is necessary to examine in some detail a terrible paradox which he believes is entailed by any attempt to give life ultimate significance. This is that every attempt to do so must end by producing the very despair that it was intended to forestall. The best way of understanding this paradox is by considering briefly a work in which Santayana used the dramatic idiom in order to highlight the underlying egotism of the moralist position.

In 1899 Santayana published a play which expressed in theatrical form his basic vision of life. It was called *Lucifer*, and was subtitled *A Theological Tragedy*. He described it as 'a philosophy conveyed in an image'. Of the many issues explored in this play, which is rich in symbolic significance, only one will be considered here. This concerns the nature of the sin which led to Lucifer's fall from grace. The paradox which Santayana wishes to stress is that the sin comes not from wickedness, but from what seems at first to be the very nobility of Lucifer's character. For Lucifer, only an absolutely good universe would be rationally acceptable: he cannot tolerate imperfection. Lucifer's real sin, in a word, is moralism, in a form so extreme that it results in a radical challenge to the very conditions of finite existence. It is the insanity of this challenge, which will not permit him to accept the limitations inherent in the act of creation, that brings Lucifer into conflict with God. Lucifer's insistence on absolute perfection entails, in short, not merely that he should be self-created, but that he should be free from the limitations to which even God himself is subject, since they are inherent in all existence. Unlike Lucifer, God accepts these limitations as inescapable. Ironically, that is, God can accept his own imperfection, and consequently rejects the quest for moral absolutes which produces Lucifer's nihilistic despair as soon as he realizes that the world can never live up to his standards of purity. Lucifer's seemingly admirable quest for purity and integrity thus conceals a *hubris* which condemns him to live in eternal loneliness, isolated forever on a mountain top.

Lucifer illuminates not only the destructive character of moralism, but also the condition for escaping from the nihilism inherent in it. This consists in a sense of piety which alone makes possible the acceptance of finite limits. Piety as Santayana uses the term owes nothing to conventional Christian religious sentiment. What he has in mind is rather piety in the ancient pagan sense, and more especially its Roman usage. In this sense, Santayana writes, piety 'may be said to mean man's reverent attachment to the sources of his being and the steadying of his life by that attachment' (LE 83). The great misfortune of the modern world is that this reverence for the sources of being has completely disappeared. We now have a concept of self in which reason and will are the predominant ingredients, with the result that anything which does not seem to express our reason or our will directly is deprived of intrinsic value. The traditional order, in particular, is therefore unhallowed. Piety is thus the crucial link between Santayana's general philosophy and his commitment to the local and the traditional. In its shortest form, the nature of this link is expressed in the proposition that 'Piety is the spirit's acknowledgement of its incarnation' (LE 84). The profoundly conservative implications of this position are evident in Santayana's almost Burkean description of piety as

> but the last bubble of a long fermentation in the world. If we wish to live associated with permanent racial interests we must plant ourselves on a broad historic and human foundation, we must absorb and interpret the past which has made us... This consciousness that the human spirit is derived and responsible, that all its functions are heritages and trusts, involves a sentiment of gratitude and duty which we may call piety (LE 83-84).

Piety is, above all, opposed to the quest for absolutes of any kind. It is committed, rather, to the imperfect and the relative. It is not, however, to be confused with the purely sentimental, passive, uncritical, and unimaginative frame of mind associated with pietism. In an eloquent passage, Santayana described the self-conscious, critical piety proper to an educated and civilized man. Piety, he writes,

> is never so beautiful and touching, never so thoroughly humane and invincible, as when it is joined to an impartial intellect, conscious of the relativity involved in existence and able to elude, through imaginative sympathy, the limits set to personal life by circumstance and private duty. As a man dies nobly when, awaiting his own extinction, he is interested to the last in what will continue to be the interests and joys of

others, so he is most profoundly pious who loves unreservedly a country, friends, and associations which he knows very well to be not the most beautiful on earth, and who, being wholly content in his personal capacity with his natural conditions, does not need to begrudge other things whatever speculative admiration they may truly deserve (LE 84).

Santayana concludes this passage with a brief indication of the moral ideal which is suggested by the openness in which piety issues, 'The ideal in this polyglot world', he writes 'where reason can receive only local and temporal expression is to understand all languages and to speak but one, so as to unite, in a manly fashion, comprehension with propriety' (LE 84).

What remains to be noticed is that in its complete or perfect form, piety extends far beyond the social order. In this complete form, piety has the universe for its object. Once again, it must be stressed that philosophic piety has nothing to do with Christian religious sentiment, but echoes pagan Stoic philosophy. Piety in this sense is rooted in the continuing awareness of man's dependence upon the natural order, and of the service provided by that order to many sides of his mind. In the pagan sense, it is inspired as much by an awareness of the scale, order, cruelty and beauty of the universe as by a sense of its benignity. In this form, philosophic piety is the precondition for the sense of integration with the universe which men seek. The full meaning of piety, however, cannot be made clear without examining the materialist doctrine in which Santayana roots it. This must be postponed for the moment in order to focus attention on the third source of alienation embedded in the western humanist tradition, which is the closure of experience by rationalism.

Rationalism

Rationalism, in Santayana's sense, is the characteristic western assumption that because reason seems supremely important to man, it must therefore be assumed to rule everything in the universe, ideally at least. As he remarked in one essay, 'The chief and most lasting illusion of the mind is the illusion of its own importance' (DL 44).

Santayana puts what is essentially the same thought in a slightly different form when he characterizes rationalism as the equation of reason with power. This equation may be traced back to the Greek world where it is fundamental, for example, to Aristotle's metaphysics. Specifically, the equation is made when Aristotle credits what he describes as a purely rational First Cause with a mysterious ability to generate motion towards itself in lesser things. Thereafter, Christian theology perpetuated Aristotle's tendency to credit rationality with power when it attributed creation to the operation of God's intellect. This exalted view of rationality, Santayana maintains, rests upon a fallacy which is endemic in the western philosophic tradition. The fallacy consists of converting logical principles of explanation into material causes of physical change. This fallacy has dominated the modern world in the form of the belief that man's intellect can grasp the causes of historical change, and in that way permit history to be brought under the control of the will.

In order to expose the more subtle and pervasive forms assumed by modern rationalism, however, and to illustrate the way in which it destroys natural piety and produces a paralysing guilt, Santayana felt impelled to look far beyond the relatively narrow world of ideological politics. For this purpose he turned once again to the literary form, composing what he described as a philosophical novel, *The Last Puritan* (1935).

The novel tells the story of the short life of Oliver Alden, a young American blessed with all the social, educational and material advantages of life, and with a virtuous and generous disposition. The puritan reference in the title is symbolic, in that Oliver's link with the historical Puritans is primarily a moral one: it is his inability to understand or accept anything except moral absolutes. His rationalism lies in the fact that his whole life is ruled by a more or less lukewarm desire to see his moral idealism implemented in practice.

This rationalism, Santayana writes, is the secret of Oliver's tragic life — 'the tragedy of the spirit when it's not content to understand but wishes to govern' (LP 15). More crudely, Oliver's tragedy is simply that he does not really live at all, for his rationalism is so profound that he gradually loses all contact with the passion which is the ultimate source of human existence. Natural spontaneity of any kind is alien to him, since it is experienced as incipient moral chaos. His problem, to be precise, is not that he has no emotions, but rather that they must be moralized before they become acceptable in his own eyes. Thus he can only legitimize love, for example, by presenting it to himself in the guise of duty.

With his inner life paralysed by the interaction of rationalism and moralism, it is hardly surprising to find that Oliver views the external world with increasing disillusion. He identifies with Hamlet, in whom he recognizes a fellow spirit, sensitive and intelligent like himself, but condemned to live an absurd life in a corrupt and intractable world. To a practical and virile eye like that of Oliver's friend Lord Jim (modelled on Earl Russell), *Hamlet* is just the story of a clever chap who was nevertheless a disaster — a chap who 'was rather a muff at love and at politics, saw a ghost, and pretended to be mad in order to hide the fact that he was a quitter' (LP 286). Oliver, of course, resents this dismissive attitude towards Hamlet's irresolution and soliloquising. Hamlet, he explains to Lord Jim, was brave and firm once he had convinced himself that he was morally in the right. If he dithered in between times, he should be admired rather than criticised for his noble regard for purity and authenticity. It was entirely natural that such moral discernment should leave him quite unfit for life in the vulgar, everyday world of ordinary mortals. In Oliver's eyes, then, Hamlet's paralysis typifies the inevitable fate that awaits anyone whose vision is sufficiently profound to create an awareness of 'how one-sided and wicked were all the principles that governed [human society]' (LP 287).

The idealism which makes Oliver's personal existence so arid issues, in public life, in a predilection for ideological politics. Since Oliver's world is one of moral absolutes, compromise of any kind is alien to him. Although in practice his conduct is entirely moderate, his moderation is not principled or stable, since it always remains completely at odds with the radical sympathies towards which his rootless idealism inevitably points. This latent radicalism is evident, for example, in the character of his nationalism. It is quite natural that as an American Oliver should love his native land; but what Santayana wishes to bring out is the fact that Oliver cannot be content with this. He cannot be content because he must 'absolutize' his patriotism, by presenting the American way of life as the only fully rational and valid mode of existence. More generally, he admires the American way because it reflects his own mentality, which is that of the modernizer, able to value only what is the direct product of conscious reason and will, and totally devoid of the piety which sympathizes with what is not of human making. For him, American superiority lies in American newness: 'Hadn't it been established in the full light of experience and reason, all the rubbish of ages cleared away, all the superfluous fat of old human nature worked off and reduced to clean hard muscle? Such a country stood on an unrivalled eminence....' (LP 290).

Not surprisingly, this admiration for an ideological politics of will and purpose, hostile as it is to compromise, tradition, and everything unplanned, gives Oliver a sneaking sympathy for Bolshevism. Although he feels his duty is to democracy, his identification of the self with the will fosters a desire to control and shape things which leaves him out of sympathy with the chaos which democracy seems to entail. As a result, he falls inevitably into the Rousseauian paradox, according to which a love of absolute liberty entails absolute surrender to the uniformity of the General Will; 'free, rare and delicate soul as he was, he would have accepted for himself this red communist tyranny that puts a grimy revolver to our noses and growls: "Be like me, or die"' (LP 13).

But the great question still remains to be answered: what does Santayana think happens to a modern romantic, idealistic, and deeply self-divided man like Oliver? Ironically, having survived the war, Oliver is killed in a motoring accident only three days after the Armistice. To regard this as a tragic waste of a young life, however, would be mistaken, in Santayana's view. It is, rather, a merciful release, since the truth of the matter is that, even before his premature death, Oliver had already suffered the fate of modern man: he was, as Santayana puts it 'played out' (LP 701). Had he lived, his life would simply have been the story of waiting told by Beckett. His character, imbued with rationalist zeal, left no room for any development, or any deepening enjoyment of life. Oliver was born already old, and his wise German governess was able to foresee his future clearly at a relatively early stage. His fate, she forecast, would be to find himself always being 'smothered by circumstances' (LP 274) in a world which refused to comply with his moral preconceptions about it.

The Last Puritan explores the ways in which the closure of experience is brought about in the course of everyday life. As the life of Oliver makes clear, modern man is unprotected against a slide into unrestrained subjectivism, the irony of which is that it is intensified by a deep regard for scientific objectivity, by a profound concern for social justice, and by a belief in the power of reason to provide a guide for authentic existence. It is, in a word, not so much the vices of modernity as its professed virtues which are the unwitting source of total world alienation.

The outcome of this alienation is a new barbarism, since civilization is identified with the existence of unacceptable external restraints upon human freedom. The precise nature of the new barbarism must, however, be explored more carefully, in order to illuminate its unique feature. This is the fact that, unlike previous barbarisms, it is not openly at odds with the external forms of civilized existence. Its essence lies not so much in outward manifestations like rape, looting and violence, as in the inward attitude to everything external which is produced by man's spiritual closure. This attitude is summarized by Santayana in the term egotism.

Egotism must not be confused with egoism. Egoism is the perfectly legitimate pursuit of its own interest in which every healthy creature engages. Egotism, in contrast, is the inability to take the independent reality of the world seriously: the world, that is, ceases to possess any genuine otherness. At first this sounds strange, as if Santayana is implausibly suggesting that men might come to think that they can walk through brick walls. What he means is rather that nothing in the external world is allowed to have any valid claim to exist except in so far as it fits in which human plans. Its value, in a word, is purely instrumental. In this sense, Oliver is obviously a supreme example of the egotistical mentality Santayana has in mind. It will be useful, however, to broaden this analysis of barbarism by considering its modern guise from a somewhat different angle. The culture of the new barbarism is essentially a culture of sovereign desire, inspired by the dream of a world in which all external obstacles to the unimpeded gratification of human wishes will eventually be removed. In this respect, the shadow which falls across modernity is the shadow of Goethe's *Faust*, who is the first truly modern man and the archetype of the new barbarism.

For Faust, Santayana maintains, gratification, in the shape of successful pursuit and enjoyment, is the yardstick by which everything is to be judged. Thus Faust turns, for example, from science, the greatest instrumentality of the modern world, to magic, in order to render the triumph of the will over all existence even more complete. It is in this respect that he is at once the first truly modern man and the first of the new barbarians, rejecting not only the limits imposed upon man by the classical and Christian cultural heritage, but all objective limits whatsoever.

What is instructive and prophetic about Faust is the fact that his rejection of limits takes the form, above all, of an idealisation of life in the form of raw, uneducated experience. Faust, that is, encapsulates the wholly egotistical spirit of modern natural man. Previously, natural man had immediately been identified as the greatest enemy of civilized life. Thus Hobbes, for example, had graphically portrayed the state of nature which he inhabits as a state of war. In some respects, the Hobbesian picture is obviously unsatisfactory, as when Hobbes assumes, for example, that the life of natural man will inevitably be poor and short: but deficiencies like that are by the way. What matters is that Hobbes took for granted that natural man wanted to be civilized, could he but find the means. This assumption was subsequently accepted by Locke, and thereafter by the eighteenth century at large. Even Rousseau visualized the civilizing of natural man through the creation of a general will.

It is in this context of traditional commitment to civilized values that Goethe's *Faust* marks a major turning point in the western attitude towards barbarism. *Faust* is, in effect, the first unqualified idealization of natural man, celebrating uncritically the pursuit of experience in any and every form, and displaying with relentless clarity the connection between egotism and barbarism. It will be objected, however, that Santayana's indictment of Faust as the archetypical new barbarian is manifestly in conflict with the end of the story, when Faust apparently adopts a life of social altruism and political responsibility that is diametrically opposed to barbaric egoism.

Looking down at the coast of Holland from a mountain top, Faust is dismayed to see the shore constantly rendered brackish and uninhabitable by the daily tides. He now conceives what is to prove his last great exploit, which is to reclaim the shore and establish a prosperous city. Surely, it might seem, this is a noble and profoundly civilized project, untainted by any trace of barbarism. In pursuing it, Faust appears finally to achieve moral maturity and a sense of deep social responsibility, so that the story as a whole is one of progress from self-indulgent egotism to wisdom. To this Santayana responds with a categorical denial: Faust remains for him a new barbarian to the last. The evidence for his unregenerate spiritual condition is to be found partly in his motive for turning to politics, and partly in the manner in which he subsequently carries out his political project.

Why, Santayana asks rhetorically, does Faust turn to politics? It is because his latest adventure with Mephistopheles has just ended, and he is therefore threatened once again by the great fear of modern man, which is the prospect of restlessness and boredom. Faust accordingly turns to politics simply 'because he must do something; and his only idea of what he hopes to secure for his subjects is that they shall always have something to do'. He has nothing better to offer, in other words, than the endless political activism which is the characteristic expression of the new barbarism. His seeming social concern is inspired by no genuine sympathy for the citizens, but only by a desire to impose on them whatever he feels is for their good, regardless of whether they themselves even want it. Just as he had no conscience when in love, he has now no conscience in his politics: his aim is only that his will should be done, and 'he does not ask whether, judged by its fruit, it will be worth doing'. His personality, Santayana concludes, has therefore not really changed at all: if he has changed his objectives it is not because his will has been educated and matured by experience, but simply because the passions of youth have been replaced by the passions of age.

Two features in particular of Faust's political style lend further support to Santayana's interpretation of his life as consistent to the end in its exemplification of the new barbarism. One is that Faust continues to rely on magic in order to ensure absolute domination of his will over nature. When the dykes and canals necessary to drain the site for his city are constructed, for example, the digging and building are done by spirits who are commanded by Mephistopheles with strange incantations. The other evidence of Faust's unregenerate nature furnished by his political style is his capacity for immoral, and even criminal, conduct. This evidence is provided by, above all, the fate of Philemon and Baucis, a fate which deserves to be recorded in full, in view of the uncannily prophetic insight it contains into what was to happen in the twentieth century, when states actually did become vehicles for the grand plans of the new barbarism. Santayana summarizes the episode as follows:

> On some sand-dunes that diversified the original beach, an old man and his wife, Philemon and Baucis, lived before the advent of Faust and his improvements. On the hillock, beside their cottage, there stood a small chapel, with a bell which disturbed Faust in his newly built palace, partly by its importunate sound, partly by its Christian suggestions, and partly by reminding him that he was not master of the country altogether, and that something existed in it not the product of his magical will. The old people would not sell out; and in a fit of impatience Faust orders that they should be evicted by force, and transferred to a better dwelling elsewhere. Mephistopheles and his minions execute these orders somewhat roughly: the cottage and chapel are set on fire, and Philemon and Baucis are consumed in the flames, or buried in the ruins.

Santayana concludes this episode by remarking ironically that although Faust expresses regret for the accident, 'it is one of those inevitable developments of action which a brave man must face, and forget as soon as possible' (LE 196-199). Faust does in fact banish his regret quite easily.

The new barbarism, then, is rendered destructive not only by the all-embracing idealism which characterized Oliver's life, but also by the relentless quest for novelty which consumes Faust. The result of combining the two images of *The Last Puritan* and *Faust* is the portrait of an age constantly threatened, on the one hand, by feelings of emotional and spiritual emptiness of the kind Oliver experiences; and no less threatened, on the other, by the prospect of life without any stable moral identity, any constitutional commitment, any sense of intrinsically significant activity, or any capacity for converting experience into wisdom, as the character of Faust makes clear.

* * * * * * * * *

Such, in outline, is Santayana's version of the alienation of modern man caused by the disintegration of the humanist tradition and the concomitant closure of the modern mind. It is time now to stand back for a moment in order to examine some of the more obvious difficulties presented by this vision. The most obvious of these concerns Santayana's account of the historical causes of alienation. This account is crucial, since before anything can be done about the alienation of the modern world, it is first necessary to determine how deeply rooted it is. Unfortunately, it must be said immediately that Santayana's account is often fanciful and unconvincing.

The focal point of Santayana's historical interpretation is the advent of a phenomenon he calls heathenism. Heathenism did not exist in ancient pagan culture, but appeared only later, with the Teutonic invasions of the Roman Empire. The essence of the heathenism which the barbarians brought with them was contained in their religion, which was simply 'the religion of will, the faith which life has in itself because it is life, and in its aims because it is pursuing them' (EGP

The Crisis of Western Humanism 43

149). This heathen religion was marked, above all, by hostility to education, discipline, and happiness — to everything, that is, for which classical pagan culture stands. In place of educated judgment it puts subjective commitment; in place of discipline it puts the unrestrained pursuit of desire; and in place of happiness it puts forward a harsh ideal of domination over everything external. Obviously, heathenism is the historic force assumed by the unrestrained egotism already discerned. The consequent problem is to determine what historical evidence there is to substantiate Santayana's belief that the barbarian invasions were in fact responsible for a major shift towards egotism in the culture of western Europe.

The principal objection to such a view is that the barbarians, far from introducing a major shift of any kind, rapidly fell under the influence of classical and Christian culture. That influence was sufficiently great, at any rate, to ensure that it is impossible to find conclusive evidence during the middle ages of the spread of anything which can be distinctively identified as a religion, or philosophy, of heathenism. To define heathenism, as Santayana does, in terms of a wilful rejection of all external limits, is so vague that it can be found in some aspect of every culture, at any period in history. Santayana himself acknowledged, for example, that wilfulness in his broad sense can be ascribed to early Hebraism, which 'regarded its tribal and moral interests as absolute, and the Creator as the champion and omnipotent agent of Israel'. This 'arrogance and inexperience', he observes, rendered the early Hebrews 'heathen' in his sense, no matter how God-fearing they might profess to be. In due course, however, the Hebrews came to accept external limits upon the will, thereby ceasing to be heathen. This occurred as soon as 'the ascendency of Israel over nature and history was proclaimed to be conditional on their fidelity to the Law'. The Hebrews finally triumphed over heathenism when 'the spirit of the nature under chastisement became more and more penitential, [and] was absorbed increasingly in the praise of wisdom. Salvation was to come only by repentance, by being born again with a will wholly transformed and broken'. The outcome was that 'the later Jewish religion went almost as far as Platonism or Christianity in the direction opposite to heathenism' (EGP 146). The trouble with this kind of historical interpretation is that it relies on impressionistic techniques which could be used to establish any number of conflicting interpretations. Santayana could, had he so wished, just as easily have presented later Hebrew history in terms of a deepening of heathenism, rather than as a movement away from it. To do so, it would only have been necessary to stress, for example, the times when the Hebrews despaired of divine assistance, and to cite the caustic admonitions of the prophets.

Given the impressionistic nature of his historical method, it is hardly surprising to find that Santayana is undeterred by the lack of concrete evidence for the spread of heathenism in the modern world. Somewhat perversely, he even tries to turn this to his advantage. There is of course no evidence of a heathen philosophy of will during the medieval period, he writes, for two reasons. One is that barbarians, by definition, are for a long time in no position to intellectualize their own barbaric view of life. But in that case, of course, it is possible to treat them like a ventriloquist's dummy, using the absence of evidence to interpret their mute lives just as one wishes. The other reason Santayana gives for remaining impervious to the lack of adequate evidence is the fact that, when barbarians do finally voice their thought, they use the language of established intellectual traditions, with the result that the novelty of their ideas is stifled. But if it is stifled what entitles Santayana to such confidence in his own interpretation of admittedly indiscernible ideas? The answer can only be in terms of the substitution of dogmatism for scholarly accuracy.

The genealogy which Santayana attributes to heathenism becomes rather less patently fanciful, however, when he jumps a thousand years and switches the quest for its origin from the barbarian invasions to the Reformation. In the Protestantism of the Reformation, Santayana maintains, 'The rebellion of the heathen soul against civilization is unmistakable' (EGP 151). But what, we must ask, is so unmistakenly heathen about Protestantism? It is the fact, Santayana replies, that 'it builds on conscience, on an emotional freedom deeply respecting itself but scarcely deciphering its purposes'; that it is 'averse to definitions and externalities of any kind'; and that 'it rejects the unworldly, disenchanted and ascetic mood of the gospel in favour of worldly success and prosperity' (LE 81).

Even if all this is granted, it scarcely suffices to convict the Reformation of introducing an unbridled cult of egotism. When the concept of will entered Reformation theology, the dispute surrounded the importance of works as a means of securing salvation, and hardly took the form of mistaking 'vitality' for 'spirituality', as Santayana suggests (LE 80). These would seem to be the polemical sentiments of a defender of orthodox Catholicism, rather than those of an impartial intellectual historian. Perhaps Santayana's most wildly unhistorical generalization, however, is his description of Protestantism as 'the religion of a race young, wistful, and adventurous, feeling its latent potentialities, vaguely assured of a worthy vocation, and possessing, like the barbarian and the healthy child, pure but unchastened energies' (LE 82). It is true that the Reformation began in Germany, but the religious ideas involved cannot be made intelligible in racial terms. Their appeal extended far beyond German frontiers, and their dissemination owed far more to political than to putative racial considerations.

If we turn now from the religious to the philosophical ideas which Santayana associates with heathenism, then his historical interpretation is no more satisfactory. He attempts, for example, to present the whole German philosophical tradition from Leibniz to Nietzsche in racial terms, as the mature expression of the world view of the Teutonic invaders. But a thinker like Hegel, it might plausibly be held, owes at least as much to Aristotle and the classical heritage as to any supposedly 'Teutonic' mode of thought. Even more serious is Santayana's interpretation of the whole of the German philosophic tradition in terms of the triumph of heathenism in the guise of subjective egotism.

Quite rightly, critics have not been slow to defend the German tradition against this interpretation. Santayana, they observe, fails to credit German philosophers like Kant, Fichte, and Hegel with making a fundamental distinction between the empirical, personal, and private self, on the one hand, and the impersonal, absolute, or transcendental ego, on the other. This latter ego, being wholly impersonal, critics observe, cannot intelligibly be accused of the extreme egotism that Santayana castigates. In Santayana's favour, however, it may be replied that his primary stress is on the *instrumental* character of German philosophy, which finds the world unintelligible unless it contributes in some way to what is seen as the development of spirit. In this sense, it remains egotistical, even when the ego in question is no longer that of an individual human being.

Nevertheless, the technique which Santayana uses to convict the German idealist philosophers is undoubtedly high-handed, being at bottom little more than the arbitrary construction of a rogues' gallery. Needless to say, the same technique could be used to assemble an entirely different collection of rogues, if different prejudices should require it. Thus Santayana's younger British contemporary, R.G.Collingwood, who shared Santayana's vision of a morally fragmented world, cast as his villains British empirical philosophers from Hobbes to Russell.

There is, however, a second major problem to be noticed in connection with Santayana's critique of modernity. This is that the critique appears at times to depend heavily upon the familiar nostalgia of conservative intellectuals who find themselves confronted by mass society for a lost golden age of organic integration between man, society, and the world. This romantic flight from the present, unsympathetic readers may complain, not only underlies Santayana's philosophic analysis of the closure of the modern mind, but also gives a utopian dimension to the ideal of openness which he opposes to it.

There is, it may immediately be granted, considerable justification for this misgiving, especially as it relates to Santayana's admiration for the supposed openness of pre-Socratic culture, and to his attempt to differentiate 'classic' and 'romantic' strands and eras in western culture. On Santayana's behalf, however, it may be replied that his philosophic position is far too subtle to be reducible to a black and white contrast between a lost world of classical restraint and a modern culture of wholesale egotism. To identify the past as a lost organic order, he is careful to insist, would be foolish in the extreme, since 'The classic and Christian synthesis from which we have broken loose was certainly premature' (SCW 10). It was premature, because that synthesis was vitiated, as has been seen, by the closure imposed upon experience by realism, moralism, and rationalism.

Just as Santayana refuses to retreat into a past golden age, so he also refuses to portray modernity as an era of unrelieved barbarism. The ascendency of egotism which characterises it, he acknowledges, has at least two positive dimensions. In the first place, it is a healthy phenomenon in so far as it entails the salutary demand that all our conventional hopes and assumptions should be called into question and tested by an appeal to experience. And secondly, it is healthy in the further sense that it makes modern experience more comprehensive. Every age tends to ignore or suppress areas of experience which lie outside conventional approval, and the egotistical quest for novelty and variety often involves a rediscovery, and perhaps a rehabilitation, of those outlawed zones.

In short, the romantic iconoclasm which Santayana castigates as heathenism is acknowledged to be commendable, in so far as it turns man back upon himself and compels him to rethink life on the basis of a deeper contact with reality. Thus, far from being an unmitigated disaster, the disintegration of humanism provides an unprecedented opportunity for creating a more profound and stable synthesis of experience than has so far been achieved in the West. To respond to the contemporary situation with the sense of disillusion and meaninglessness that has frequently characterized the present century is therefore inappropriate. Before Santayana's own mood of measured affirmation can be shared, however, it is necessary to consider more carefully what he believes to be the fundamental conditions for the achievement of a deeper synthesis of experience. These conditions may be summarized as a philosophy of naturalism. It is therefore to the meaning of Santayana's naturalism that we must now turn.

Chapter 3: Towards a new synthesis: the philosophy of naturalism

Faced by the disintegration of all traditional beliefs, the great task of the modern world is to construct a new synthesis of experience. The problem, however, is to decide what resources are available for this task, in view of the limitations of the western humanist tradition described in the previous chapter. Santayana's reply is that they are provided by what he terms a philosophy of naturalism.

The full meaning of naturalism can only be explained by outlining the philosophy itself, but the point of the term is to emphasise that it is a philosophy founded exclusively upon human nature and the human condition. The 'message' of this philosophy, as Santayana put it, is 'that morality and religion are expressions of human nature; that human nature is a biological growth; and finally that spirit, fascinated and tortured, is involved in the process, and asks to be saved' (PGS 23).

The significance of this message consists, in particular, in the fact that the ideal of spiritual

which inspires it rests upon a more balanced, lucid and comprehensive view of the human condition than is possible within either of the two one-sided traditions of thought which have dominated western speculation. The first is idealism, which tends to endow man with an exaggerated spirituality, and therefore to give inadequate attention to the actual structure of the material universe which he inhabits. The other is materialism, which concentrates on the tangible facts of human existence at the expense of ignoring the spiritual dimension of human nature.

A naturalist philosophy, then, attempts in effect to balance a sense of man's ideal possibilities against awareness of the inescapability of human imperfection.

From this point of view, the message of naturalism may be reformulated in terms of what Santayana calls the life of reason. The essence of the life of reason is the recognition that compromise and moderation are the necessary conditions of civilized existence. The life of reason seeks, in particular, to secure the middle ground — the most precarious part of modern life — against the two extremes which have threatened it during the past two centuries. One of these extremes is the spirit of anarchic individualism; the other is the utopian vision of community inspired by collectivist ideologies.

To state the aim of naturalism in general terms is easy enough; to identify in detail the exact nature of the foundations upon which the new naturalist synthesis of experience might be constructed, however, is an altogether more difficult enterprise. Taking Santayana's writings as a whole, three interlocking foundations may be discerned.

The first foundation consists of philosophic laughter or, more precisely, of the comic vision. The second is a materialist theory of rationality. Although Santayana is a critic of the materialism of our age, the concept of spirituality which he opposes to it is based on a more profound materialism, rather than on the rejection of it.

The third foundation is a sceptical method which involves more, however, than a mere intellectual technique. It is, indeed, nothing less than the door which, when opened, reveals the dimension of the self and the world that a predominantly instrumental culture inevitably obscures from men. The sceptical method aims, in short, at spiritual emancipation, rather than at mere intellectual subversion.

In order to determine the overall coherence of Santayana's philosophy, it is necessary to begin by looking at each of the three foundations in more detail.

The comic vision

By placing laughter at the very centre of his philosophy, Santayana immediately strikes a note which is alien to most modern thought. He also runs the risk of being accused of frivolity. The kind of laughter he has in mind, however, is not frivolous, but is, on the contrary, the only means of creating the pre-condition for lucid philosophising about the human condition. This is intellectual humility.

Why laughter alone can perform this function will become apparent if we recall once again the central assumption of the western intellectual tradition, which is that man occupies a privileged position in the universe, in relation to which everything else in the order of being possesses only an instrumental value. To achieve a less arrogant philosophic vantage-point, rational argument alone will not suffice, since the origin of anthropocentrism lies in human vanity. The only effective antidote for the intense egoism which lies behind this vanity is laughter. 'Against evils born of pure vanity and self-deception', Santayana writes, and in particular 'against the verbiage by which man persuades himself that he is the goal and acme of the universe, laughter is the proper defence' (LE 228).

Laughter is crucial, however, not only as a means of eliminating the distortion of perspective caused by the arrogance of anthropocentrism, but also to enable men to confront the most unpalatable feature of existence. This is its intrinsic meaninglessness. Existence, Santayana writes, 'is contingency and absurdity incarnate, the oddest of possibilities masquerading momentarily as a fact' (SE 142). The meaninglessness and absurdity of existence need not, however, be a source of pain to man. They may instead be a source of joyful affirmation. The path from angst to joy will begin to emerge if we recall for a moment the Dionysiac sense of delight generated by participation in a carnival.

The carnival image, Santayana believes, is in fact the one in which the comic vision of existence is most faithfully expressed (SE 139). What, he asks rhetorically, could be more exhilarating than the image of existence as a rout? Such an image appeals, above all, to the non-instrumental, sportive side of man's nature, 'itself akin to a shower of sparks and a pattern of irrevocable adventures.' The art of life, he continues, 'is to keep step with the celestial orchestra that beats the measure of our cares, and gives the cue for our exists and our entrances.... It is a great Carnival, and amongst these lights and shadows of comedy, these roses and vices of the playhouse, there is no abiding' (SE 144).

The possibility that existence is intrinsically comic, however, is something that can only be contemplated in a philosophic tradition characterized by the intellectual humility just mentioned. It is therefore a possibility which has seldom occurred to western philosophers, who have arrogantly preferred to believe that just because they themselves are without a trace of humour, the universe too must be without one (SE 14). Accordingly, they long ago devised a simple but ingenious strategy by which to support their solemn pretensions. From Plato onwards, they have asserted that existence is an illusion, and then concluded that true reality is therefore to be found somewhere outside the world that actually exists.

In retrospect, the disastrous outcome of this strategy is all too obvious: without realizing it, western thinkers have systematically inflicted upon themselves a condition of world-alienation, under the mistaken impression that such alienation is inherent in the human condition. A little humility would have nipped this unhappy development in the bud, by enabling them to celebrate the idea of an absurd universe; but such humility is impossible, it can now be seen, unless philosophy is founded upon the laughter which western philosophers have always despised.

It may still be felt, however, that laughter, no matter how philosophic it maybe, reveals a deplorable indifference to the sufferings of mankind. But that is not so. What the comic vision nurtures is a deepened sympathy for human suffering, rather than a complacent indifference to it. This seeming paradox is easily explained by recalling that the great radical ideologies of the modern world, all of which set out to eliminate suffering, have not only ended by increasing it, but have adamantly denied their responsibility for doing so.

This perversity is familiar, for example, in the form of the Marxist belief that those who claim to know the meaning of history are entitled to inflict untold suffering upon their opponents whom they dismiss as reactionary enemies of the proletariat. It is in moral fervour of this kind, rather than in the humility fostered by the comic vision, that contempt for suffering is bred. Such contempt is quite alien to the philosophic laughter which Santayana has in mind, for this always has in it 'an overtone of sympathy and brotherly understanding; as the laughter which greets Don Quixote's absurdities and misadventures does not mock the hero's intent [but only his failure to accept that] the world must be known before it can be reformed' (LE 228).

Like every other perspective, however, the comic vision has only a conditional (and therefore limited) validity. Although Santayana regards it as uniquely appropriate in philosophy, where it is the only effective means of demolishing intellectual vanity, he explicitly recognizes that life may also be seen in tragic terms. The tragic vision, however, only emerges when existence is no longer viewed contemplatively, as it is by the philosopher, but is seen instead from the standpoint of participants who have inflexibly committed themselves to preserving their identity in the face of insuperable obstacles. As Santayana puts it, 'Every one who is sure of his mind, or proud of his office, or anxious about his duty, assumes a tragic mask. He deputes it to be himself and transfers to it almost all his vanity' (LE 133-4). All that matters at present, however, is that *for the philosopher,* to begin and end with laughter is the only sure means of preserving the sense of modesty which is the basis of intellectual sanity. Laughter, in a word, is the key to maintaining a sense of what Santayana calls 'the human scale' in human imagination and action.

Materialism

In order to reinforce the sense of intellectual humility fostered by the comic vision, it is necessary to supplement the rejection of anthropocentrism with a critique of the excessively spiritual interpretation of human nature inspired by the Platonic and Christian view of man.

This exaggerated sense of human spirituality is the source, above all, of the extraordinary piece of fantasy which has inspired liberal democratic culture since the emergence of activist politics at the time of the French Revolution. The essence of this fantasy is the belief that the self is a wholly indeterminate entity with limitless possibilities and equally limitless capabilities. These limitless possibilities and capabilities, modern progressive orthodoxy holds, are systematically obstructed by the existing social order. Radical change, it is believed, will unlock these stifled capabilities and automatically produce liberty and peace.

A more adequate concept of the self, Santayana suggests, is intimated by the Indian doctrine of Karma, which is diametrically opposed to the modern western concept of the indeterminate self. In Indian philosophy, every self has a definite heritage, an imposed character, and a specific task assigned to it. Wisdom is only achieved, Indian philosophy holds, when this task is discovered, readily accepted, and completely carried out. Indian wisdom is therefore directly opposed to western folly, which imagines that 'any scent is worth following, that we have an infinite nature, or no nature in particular, that life begins without obligation and can do business without capital, and that the will is vacuously free' (FE 99-100).

Since the doctrine of Karma belongs to a different cultural tradition, however, it can of course do no more than point out the direction in which contemporary western thought needs to move; the question remains open as to whether the western tradition itself contains any means of overcoming the destructive ideal of the indeterminate self. In the work of Freud in particular, Santayana found a welcome indication that a positive answer to this problem might be possible. He sympathized, in particular, with Freud's analysis of the deep animal roots upon which the seemingly autonomous ego is dependent. In the end, however, Santayana considered that a fully coherent account of human nature requires a more philosophical approach than psycho-analysis can provide. Within the western intellectual tradition, he believed, materialist philosophy provides the only satisfactory foundation for such an approach. To devise a form of materialism which formulates the relation between mind and matter in an adequate fashion is therefore one of his principal concerns.

During the past century the best-known version of materialism has been Marxism. Santayana's objection to Marxism, however, is that it has only ever been materialist in name; in practice, Marxism has always been ready to abandon the logic of materialist philosophy in favour of an extravagant humanist dream of liberation through revolutionary change.

In order to find a satisfactory version of materialism, then, it is necessary to go beyond Marxism. Santayana had no hesitation about the direction in which to look. He turned first of all to Lucretius, as the philosopher who mounted, if not the first, at least the most sustained attack upon the Socratic tradition of humanist philosophy to be found in western thought prior to the modern period. Amongst modern philosophers he admired Spinoza above all others, on the ground that he has gone furthest in rejecting the excessive spirituality of the Platonic and Christian view of man.

Of these two great materialist philosophers, it was Lucretius who impressed Santayana most. This may seem surprising, since Lucretius' *De Rerum Natura* is now generally dismissed as merely a crude, albeit poetic and imaginative, anticipation of modern atomic theory. For Santayana, however, Lucretius' true significance lies at a far more profound level. It consists, more precisely, in a concept of the self — or, less anachronistically, of what the ancient Romans called the *anima*, or soul — which is completely different from the concept with which the modern world is familiar.

Ever since the time of Descartes, the self has been identified with consciousness, in a sense which drives a wedge between consciousness and the matter upon which it depends. The ancient world, by contrast, identified the self not with consciousness, but with a material essence which not only governed the formation of the body, but also warmed, moved and guided it. In Lucretius' philosophy, this material essence is conceived to be a swarm of very small volatile atoms, 'a sort of ether, resident in all living souls, breathed in abundantly during life and breathed out at death' (TPP 49-50).

The fact that this conceptualization of the self may now seem to us simple and crude, Santayana insists, is beside the point. What is noteworthy is that Lucretius rejected the prevailing metaphysical explanation of the universe. He refused, that is, to follow the Socratic tradition of projecting human ideals on to the world, in a way which obscures the natural self and its roots in the physical order of being that nourishes it. In short, crude though Lucretius's atomism may be, it has the great merit of firmly relocating man within the natural world. By making spirit inseparable from its physical embodiment, it re-establishes the continuity of human nature with that of the universe. Unlike Plato and his disciples, Lucretius therefore had no misgivings about a universe which is indifferent to man, which is why he felt no need to take refuge in the illusory consolation of metaphysics.

In this respect, Santayana maintains, materialism is the only truly solid and genuine foundation for human dignity. The moralistic concept of dignity with which Christianity, following in the footsteps of Plato, has familiarized us is a sham, in so far as it fosters comforting human sentiments which are not grounded in the material structure of being. Lucretius' concept of dignity, by contrast, is rooted in a combination of lucidity and intellectual modesty which accepts the undistorted facts of existence, just as they are. Confronted by a disenchanted world, that is to say, Lucretius does not seek re-enchantment by retreating into the past, or into a world of myth. Instead, he finds a new source of enchantment at the heart of disenchantment itself, through the joy borne of lucidity.

In the end, however, Lucretius did not manage to avoid an error which, Santayana maintains, has continued to vitiate the entire western materialist tradition down to the present day. This consists of maintaining that only matter is ultimately real. The result, as the cruder forms of Marxism have made only too clear, is an epiphenomenalist doctrine in which the world of spirit is dismissed as mere appearance, without any attempt to do justice to morality, politics, religion and art on their own terms.

What Santayana's revised version of materialism maintains, by contrast, is not that matter alone is real, but that only matter exists (PGS 509). What is meant by saying that only matter exists, Santayana explains, is that matter alone can exercise power within the causal order of the universe. Man, in so far as his being is rooted in what Santayana describes as the physical order of the psyche, belongs

Towards a new synthesis: the philosophy of naturalism

to the causal world; but in so far as he is capable of spiritual life, he is independent of it, since spirit takes him into a world of creative (or autonomous) imagination. Thus we are able to listen to music, for example, because we are spiritual beings; but we could not hear the music without a psyche whose physical organs are responsive to the stimuli provided by sound. We can, however, enjoy music perfectly well without every being conscious of the physical vibration caused by sound on our eardrums. Nevertheless, the independence of the spirit from the material world is never total: spirit in man always remains dependent upon and conditioned by the material needs and interests of the psyche in which it is rooted.

The identification of the self with the psyche imposes a salutary limitation upon the unlimited flights of fancy to which the concept of the indeterminate self otherwise leaves men prone. As Santayana puts it, 'consciousness was created by the muses; but meantime industrious nature, in our bodily organization, takes good care to keep our actions moderately sane, in spite of our poetic genius' (PGS 29). The parallel noticeable here with the Marxist theory of consciousness will not be found surprising if it is remembered that Santayana was not opposed in principle to the materialist side of that doctrine.

Santayana's attempts to formulate materialism in a way which asserts the causal primacy of the physical world, on the one hand, whilst simultaneously acknowledging the autonomy of the spiritual world, on the other, raises many problems. Santayana himself was profoundly aware of this, and was prepared to admit that all the main criticisms were likely to have some justification. Nevertheless, he ultimately dismissed them as mistaken. They are mistaken, he said, because they assume that his materialism, like that of other materialist philosophers, is intended to be taken as a literal description of the universe. In view of his insistence that any literal interpretation of his doctrine is a misinterpretation, it is clearly necessary to consider exactly what Santayana believes the status of a truly naturalistic philosophy to be.

Santayana's response to the question is to explain that 'My naturalism or materialism is no academic opinion…it [is rather] an everyday conviction which came to me...from experience and observation of the world at large, and especially of my own feelings and passions. It seems to me', he continues, 'that those who are not materialists cannot be good observers of themselves: they may hear themselves thinking, but they cannot have watched themselves acting and feeling, for feeling and action are evidently accidents of matter...' (PGS 12).

Materialism in this sense, then, is intended to be no more than a fundamentally untechnical attempt to stick to what common sense teaches everyone. Because it is firmly rooted in common sense, it is unaffected by, for example, what the latest scientific discoveries tell us about the nature of matter. What the physicists and chemists say has no relevance, since the primary concern of common sense materialism is ethical. It does not aim, that is, at a literal description of the external world, but at pragmatically identifying the conditions of human happiness (PGS 12-13). If it is asked precisely what a literal description of the world involves, Santayana's reply is that 'it would be found only, perhaps, in literature — in the reproduction of discourse by discourse' (OS 177).

In the present context, however, what requires to be considered immediately is what Santayana regards as the most important of the conditions for the happiness just referred to. This is the need to control an illusion which is inherent in the very nature of human existence, and to which every human being is therefore automatically prone. The illusion in question is the belief that the self is synonymous with the conscious, rational, and seemingly autonomous ego with which we automatically identify ourselves so long as we enjoy good health, full stomachs, and agreeable surroundings. We are all, that is to say, prone to think of ourselves in Cartesian terms, so long as nothing impinges upon the body, either internally or externally, to force awareness of the corporality of spirit upon us.

At first sight, the illusion of spiritual autonomy might seem to be a matter of little practical consequence, important only as a topic for specialized philosophic debates about the mind-body relation. For Santayana, however, it is the main reason for rejecting the idea which inspires all modern radical thought: the belief, namely, that the origin of evil lies in the structure of society, from which the conclusion is drawn that man may be liberated by radical social and political change. The utopian character of this optimistic view becomes apparent as soon as it is realized that the illusion of spiritual autonomy is in fact a form of madness.

Santayana had already connected the ideas of pure spirituality, absolute autonomy and madness in his early play, *Lucifer*, as was previously noticed, but at that stage he had treated madness as an exceptional condition. With the publication of *Dialogues in Limbo*, however, he identified a propensity to madness as the universal condition of mankind.

In a dialogue with the title 'Normal Madness', for example, Democritus maintains that: 'Of life madness is an inseparable and sometimes predominant part' (DL 41). Everybody, he insists, is inevitably mad, because he makes his own consciousness an absolute reference point in determining what is to count as sanity or normality. Fortunately, this situation is not disastrous, since 'normal' madness can pass as sanity unless it impedes action or is mistaken for the substance of the external world itself.

Specifically, Santayana observes, normal madness can pass as conventional sanity in three situations. The first is when it is restrained by institutions which render it functional, as was the case with the ancient study of omens in time of war. Although a form of madness, this practice helped to brace men for war, and its insanity therefore did not preclude it from having practical value. The second condition is when madness is shared. Agreement in madness is in fact the definition of friendship, as was explicitly recognized by the Greeks. Finally, habits and ideas will be conventionally regarded as sane if they are sanctioned by tradition (DL 46). The task, then, is not to eliminate madness from human nature: that would be impossible without destroying consciousness itself. It is, rather, to contain and channel madness in ways which make it creative, or at any rate functional. This enterprise, however, is always a precarious one, for there always remains a sort of subterranean chaos, sometimes bursting through the crust of civilization; and something in the individual heart rejoices at that eruption, feels that at last the moment has come to break through its own crust, and build itself, as well as the world, on some different plan. Not a better plan, since there is no deeper organism to pronounce on the matter or to have any stake in it; but simply a relief from this plan, from this routine and this morality, from these surroundings, and these prospects. It is what Descartes called the infinity of the will, contrasted with the finitude of reason; but perhaps we might more accurately say that it is the indetermination of matter, or of protoplasm, contrasted with the definite organisation of powers and habits in man. A sort of self-hatred and self-contempt: a wild throw for something different, and a deep, dark impulse to challenge and to destroy everything that has the impertinence to exist (DP 439-440).

Materialism, then, is not only the basis of human dignity, as Lucretius saw, but also of sanity itself. Materialism in this sense, it must be stressed once again, does not assert the unreality of spirit, but only the dependence of spirit upon matter. There is, therefore, no opposition 'between materialism and a Platonic or even Indian discipline of the spirit. The recognition of the material world and of the conditions of existence in it merely enlightens the spirit concerning the source of its troubles and the means to its happiness and deliverance... [It is this] that alone really concerned me' (PGS 12-13).

Although Santayana insisted on the untechnical, common sense character of materialism, it need hardly be said that some of the problems to which his doctrine gives rise are in fact extremely technical. One of these is to decide what the concept of matter itself means, when used in a non-literal or symbolic way.

Matter as it is in itself, Santayana maintains, can never be known to us. Our contact with it is only through its impact upon us, which we interpret according to the needs of human beings, but without ever being able to grasp what it is that ultimately impacts upon our bodies. So far as our knowledge of other human beings is concerned, the situation is no different, except that in this case our tendency to project our inner experience on to the outer world of things happens to be confirmed by their response.

The real problem presented by this common sense materialism, however, is its failure to provide a solution to the subjectivist tendency which Santayana castigates in modern culture at large.

In his first systematic presentation of his philosophy in *The Life of Reason*, this problem had been obscured by what Santayana himself subsequently rejected as an indefensibly dogmatic conception of what rationality entails. More precisely, in that work Santayana had assumed that rationality means what the Greek philosophers meant by it, and had arbitrarily assigned universal validity to this conviction.

Subsequently, Santayana moved towards a relativist position which denied that any philosophy would provide a universally valid message. Whilst this relativism made his position more consistent, it deprived his original distinction between civilization and barbarism of any philosophical foundation. That distinction had rested on his claim that the former is rational and the latter irrational; but from a relativist standpoint that distinction was no longer tenable. This, however, was not too serious a difficulty: Santayana was able to solve it by redefining civilization in terms of compromise, toleration and diversity, and barbarism as a narrow and inflexible attitude which judges everything solely by the passions, whatever they may be. What could not so easily be put right, however, was the conflict between Santayana's naturalism, on the one hand, and his desire on the other to develop a concept of absolute certainty with which to ward off the charge of radical subjectivism to which his naturalism might otherwise have left his position exposed. It is this problem which Santayana sought to confront in *Scepticism and Animal Faith* (1923), in which he outlined the foundation of his mature philosophical system.

The solution to subjectivism proposed in that work is dramatic: instead of searching for a principle which would guarantee objective certainty, as philosophers have done ever since Plato, Santayana embraced the idea that life is a dream, whilst simultaneously rejecting the seemingly inevitable conclusion that we are therefore condemned to solipsism. In order to understand how he believed that a commitment to rational inquiry could be reconciled with the vision of man as confined forever within the sphere of myth, it is necessary to examine the theory of philosophic method by means of which he attempted to provide naturalism with a completely objective epistemological foundation.

Ultimate Scepticism

In *Scepticism and Animal Faith*, Santayana observed that 'At any juncture in the life of reason a man may ask himself, as I am doing in this book, what he is most certain of.' Replying to his own question, he announced that 'I have...discovered what [the] bed-rock of perfect certitude is; somewhat disconcertingly, it turns out to be in the region of the rarest ether. I have absolute assurance of nothing, save of the character of some given essences; the rest is arbitrary belief or added by animal impulse' (SAF 110).

In order to arrive at the essences which constitute the 'bed-rock of perfect certitude,' Santayana claims, it is first necessary to realise that the nature of absolute certainty has been misunderstood by philosophers. Their mistake has been to assume that what certainty requires is knowledge which can be guaranteed to provide an accurate representation of the facts of existence. In a manner reminiscent of Hume, Santayana dismisses as absurd the idea that there can ever be knowledge of this kind, on the ground that belief in the existence of anything at all — including my own existence — is 'something radically incapable of proof' (SAF 35). What we commonly think of as certain knowledge of existence is really belief, and rests, not on knowledge, but 'on some irrational persuasion' Santayana calls animal faith.

Although animal faith has no rational foundation, it must immediately be added that it may find a pragmatic justification, in so far as its initially blind and purely impulsive character is transformed by experience into a basis for harmonious adjustment to the material world in which we live. This pragmatic certainty is neither subjective

Towards a new synthesis: the philosophy of naturalism

nor objective, since it does not involve any literal claim about the nature of the world which confronts us. What philosophers since Plato have thought of as the problem of objective certainty only arises when we forget the irrational roots of human life in animal faith and think of ourselves as purely rational beings who aspire to literal knowledge of existence. Then, and only then, does the spectre of subjectivism begin to haunt us. That spectre disappears the moment we recall the true position, which may be briefly restated as follows:

> Knowledge of existence has no need, no propensity, and no fitness to be literal. It is symbolic initially, when a sound, a smell, an indescribable feeling, are signals to the animal of his dangers or chances; and it fulfils its function perfectly — I mean its moral function of enlightening us about our natural good — if it remains symbolic to the end. Can anything be more evident than that religion, language, patriotism, love, science itself speak in symbols? (SAF 102)

This pragmatism creates a marked similarity of mood between Santayana's version of materialism and the British school of common sense philosophy originally developed by John Locke. In particular, Santayana shares Locke's conviction that their natural faculties are capable of providing human beings with all they require to live in harmony with the world (FE 6), and that only mistaken and unrealizable intellectual ambition obscures this from them. Santayana departs from the British school, however, in insisting that a common sense philosophy cannot itself be adequately defended by common sense. He is determined, above all, to go beyond the British school in demonstrating that men do not have to be content with a merely pragmatic certainty, but can achieve the absolute certainty which they have long sought, even though this proves to rest upon an entirely different foundation from the illusory knowledge of existence hitherto associated with it.

If absolute certainty has nothing to do either with knowledge, or with acquaintance with facts, how is it arrived at? In order to understand its true nature, it is necessary to adopt an extremely rigorous methodological scepticism, in the form of an imaginative act by which we strip away every belief that is merely a belief. It will immediately be objected, however, that this is far from novel, being in fact no more than what a long line of philosophers, from Socrates to Hume, have already done. Santayana, however, dismisses all these earlier versions of the sceptical method as superficial. On close inspection they all turn out to have been nothing more than intellectual devices for replacing one kind of dogmatism with another. In short, the so-called sceptical philosophers of the past were not really sceptical at all.

Consider, for example, the Socratic method, which is generally regarded as marking the birth of scepticism. It is in reality only an arbitrary way of upgrading one part of being and downgrading another. Specifically, what Socrates did was to confer the status of absolute reality on the ethical values of which he happened to approve, whilst downgrading the deliverances of the senses, of which he disapproved, to the status of appearance. In a word, his sceptical method was not really sceptical in any rigorous sense, since the ethical values he himself happened to hold were exempted from exposure to it.

Similarly, the supposedly sceptical method of universal doubt adopted in the modern world by Descartes is not really sceptical because it proves, on inspection, not to have been universal. More precisely, Descartes fell far short of what Santayana calls 'ultimate scepticism' because it never occurred to him to extend his supposedly universal method to his own principles of explanation. He never, for example, doubts the existence of a correspondence between human thought and the structure of the external world (SAF 289).

If the method of ultimate scepticism is pursued unflinchingly, what it reveals is that the only possible source of absolute certainty in experience is the intuition of essences. Essences are neither ideas, which presuppose a distinction between the knower and the known, nor mysterious metaphysical entities, as Plato considered them to be. They cannot, therefore, be properly described as either subjective or objective. They are, rather, immediately intuited constituents of consciousness, without which no discourse is possible, and no individuated existence can occur (SAF 101). It is because they are immediately intuited, and not strictly 'known', that they give absolute certainty.

Perhaps the most remarkable aspect of the doctrine of essences, however, is Santayana's seemingly paradoxical assertion that, although they are real, they do not exist. The term existence designates in this sense 'such being as is in flux, determined by external relations, and jostled by irrelevant events' (SAF 42). By maintaining that they are nevertheless real, Santayana is assigning them the kind of status enjoyed, for example, by Kant's *a priori* categories; which is to say that, although they are not themselves experienced, experience is quite impossible without them. In Santayana's philosophy, however, essences are constitutive foundations of both the world of spirit and that of matter, whereas Kant confined his *a priori* categories to the former. Essences, that is, are at once the terms used in discourse to describe the objects with whose existence animal faith acquaints us, and the source of the identity of those objects themselves. In this respect, Santayana is closer to the Platonic concept of eternal forms than to Kant's doctrine, although in his version the forms exert no power over matter, and are not restricted to the ethical ones to which Plato's attention was confined.

Santayana's search for absolute certainty presents many problems, not least of which is the potential incoherence created by introducing absolutes of any sort into a philosophy whose materialist stress appears to point to the inescapable conditionality of all experience. Other problems include the difficulty of deciding what is meant by Santayana's claim that essences are eternal; his difficulty in establishing whether we can ever be sure that we are talking about the same essence that we intuited a moment ago; and the apparent impossibility of being sure that two or more people can intelligibly be said to intuit the same essence. Such difficulties strongly suggest that the doctrine of essence is not a very satisfactory way of doing what it claims to do, which is to explain the conditions of discourse and the nature of things themselves.

The technical problems presented by the doctrine of essence, however, must not be allowed to conceal what Santayana considered to be its greatest strength. The doctrine was never intended to be merely an epistemological device for achieving absolute certainty, or an ontological construction for smoothing out difficulties peculiar to the Platonic theory of ideas. Over and beyond those dimensions the doctrine had an ethical role in his thought, and it was upon this that he laid the main emphasis.

From the ethical standpoint, the doctrine of essences is the key to an ideal of spiritual liberation which constitutes the supreme good for man. Santayana describes this liberation in the following words:

> A mind enlightened by scepticism and cured of noisy dogmas, a mind discounting all reports, and free from all tormenting anxiety about its own fortunes or existence finds in the wilderness of essence a very sweet and marvellous solitude. The ultimate reaches of doubt and renunciation open out for it, by an easy transition, into fields of endless variety and peace, as if through the gorges of death it had passed into a paradise where all things are crystallized into the image of themselves, and have lost their urgency and their venom (SAF 76).

As this passage makes clear, the complicated philosophical doctrine of essence which sustains Santayana's ideal of liberation conceals a thought which is at once ancient and simple. It is that the world cannot be wisely and truly loved unless it has first been completely renounced — a thought which is encapsulated in familiar form in, for example, the Christian doctrine that a man must lose his life in order to gain his soul. Ancient though this thought may be, however, our own century generally views it with deep suspicion, since any critique of the world of will and desire is regarded as escapist, irresponsible, or worst of all — symptomatic of libidinal deficiency.

Santayana's ideal of liberation has predictably been derided for exemplifying all these putative vices. Such criticisms, however, slide too easily over the fact that his doctrine is merely restating what western thinkers regarded as the central feature of the human condition until roughly some two centuries ago. This is the existence of an ineliminable tension between reason and desire. The stress falls on the word ineliminable. The tension itself is of course familiar to everyone, but a great divide separates those who regard it as eliminable and those who regard it as ineradicable. The particular interest of Santayana's philosophy lies in the journey he made from the former camp to the latter.

Santayana himself had begun by sharing the uncritical optimism about human perfectibility which characterized European life before 1914. In *The Life of Reason*, this optimism was reflected in an ideal of rational harmony which assumed that reason and desire can in principle be united in an organically integrated self. In the event, however, Santayana's early optimism about the possibility of unifying the divided self did not survive very long into the present century. In particular, the traumatic experience of the First World War was reflected philosophically in a gradual rejection of pagan Greek optimism about the role of reason in ethical life and a growing sympathy for Christian pessimism.

This shift of emphasis is evident, for example, in *Soliloquies in England* (1922), where Santayana asks rhetorically how reason can ever be expected to play a significant part in human affairs in a world in which even war appears to teach men nothing. The truth, it seems, is that men prefer not to live rationally, but 'moodily, in the dark' (SE 101). If they ever learn from experience, 'it is too late and to no purpose' (SE 101).

It is against the background of the war experience that Santayana's revised vision of spiritual liberation took shape. His early dream of ultimately eliminating the tension between desire and reason in an harmonious whole in which all passions and interests found room is replaced in the mature post-war doctrine by the ideal of liberation through the 'disintoxication' of desire. The meaning of disintoxication will be examined shortly. For the moment, it is necessary to consider three objections to which Santayana's vision of spiritual liberation gives rise.

The first objection is that it is not more than an intellectual veneer for what is at bottom merely a reversion to the Catholic culture in which Santayana spent his childhood. The criticism has an element of truth in it. Santayana always acknowledged his admiration for Catholicism, and readily admitted its enduring influence on his thought. His earliest speculation, he remarked, was 'philosophically religious', adding immediately, 'as it has always remained' (PGS 24). More especially, he considered that the Christian symbolism of the cross and the resurrection embodied a profound insight into the nature of life which the modern secular age finds hard to understand. What Christianity taught is that in spite of suffering, 'the world which torments us is truly beautiful...and we are not wrong in living it, but only in appropriating it' (SE 94). He accordingly preferred Christianity to Bhuddism, for 'Christ loved the world in an erotic sense in which Bhudda did not love it, and the world has therefore loved the cross as it can never love the Bo-tree' (SE 94).

In spite of his sympathy for religion, however, Santayana emphasized that the spiritual life is fundamentally different from the religious one, while simultaneously confessing his fear that his fate might be to replace Aristotle as the accepted Pagan philosopher for Catholics. Two differences which he stressed illuminate his position.

In the first place, the core of the spiritual life is disinterested contemplation of pure being. Its essence is therefore an ideal of pure detachment. Religion, however, cannot be disinterested, since it is concerned with God, and not with pure being. Unlike pure being, God is the object of desire, and therefore cannot possibly be viewed by the religious man with complete detachment. Stated more dramatically, the same point may be made by saying that God is always deemed by the religious man to exist, but that pure being, the object of the spiritual life, consists of pure essences, and therefore has being but no existence (RB 66-63).

The spiritual life is marked, secondly, by an aesthetic dimension which, while not alien to religion, is only incidental to the religious concern for personal consolation and fulfilment. Santayana is somewhat ambiguous about the aesthetic dimension of the spiritual life, since he sometimes presents spiritual detachment as so pure that even the aesthetic dimension is alien to it. It is significant, however, that he found the finest illustration of the relation between the doctrine of essence and the true meaning of spiritual liberation neither in a religious mystic nor an Indian guru, but in the work of a modern novelist.

He quotes with unqualified approval Proust's account of his personal discovery of the reality of essences in the final volume of *A la recherche du temps perdu*. The passage occurs in the course of Proust's account of how he moved from a condition in which, he wrote, he had come to find 'society and even life itself tiresome', to one in which he henceforth experienced 'an eagerness to live.' The secret, Proust explained, was a radical change in his view of life brought about by the liberating discovery that the dissatisfied being within him

> draws its sustenance only from the essence of things, in that alone does it find its nourishment and its delight... Let a sound already heard or an odour caught in bygone years be sensed anew, simultaneously in the present and the past, real without being of the present moment, ideal but not abstract, and immediately the permanent essence of things, usually concealed, is set free and our true self...awakes, takes on fresh life as it receives the celestial nourishment brought to it...This contemplation, although part of eternity, was transitory. And yet I felt that the pleasure it had bestowed on me at rare intervals in my life was the only one that was fecund and real...And so it was decided to consecrate myself to the study of the essence of things... (OS 208).

Santayana's admiration for Proust leads naturally to the second major objection which his ideal of spiritual liberation frequently encounters. This is that it is an essentially élitist affair, with no universal relevance. At the time when he wrote *The Life of Reason* Santayana would have rejected this charge, but the relativism of his mature philosophy led him to regard it more sympathetically, and yet to dismiss it as misconceived. 'I have become aware', he wrote in the preface to his main work on politics, 'that any one's sense of what is good and beautiful must have a somewhat narrow foundation, namely the circumstances of his particular brand of human nature, and he should not expect the good or the beautiful after his own heart to be greatly prevalent or long maintained' (DP vii). It follows from this general position, as he noted elsewhere, that 'the spiritual life, and the pure being to which its contemplation is addressed, can be good only in relation to the living souls that may find their good there' (PSL 46). It is therefore perfectly natural for the statesman and the father of a family, for example, to dismiss the spiritual life as 'wasteful, disruptive, and idle' (PSL 46). Accordingly, no one has any obligation to live the spiritual life. Santayana himself could therefore admit, without any inconsistency or sense of self-reproach, that he chose to pursue only a very modest version of it in his own life. 'I frankly cleave,' he remarked, 'to the Greek and not to the Indian, and I aspire to be a rational animal rather than a pure spirit' (RB 65).

Nevertheless, Santayana stressed that despite the concessions to relativism just made, the spiritual life is relevant to all men, to the extent that it is inevitably foreshadowed to some degree in every life. It is foreshadowed in the sense that every life displays at least some spontaneous, non-instrumental interest in the world. These intimations of spiritual life in ordinary experience, Santayana observes, include 'laughter, when it is not inspired by a sense of personal superiority or scorn; love, when it does not seek possession; the awareness of beauty, when it is not merely for ornament or relaxation; and prayer, when it does not merely seek to control the course of nature' (RB 746).

The worldly sympathy evident in these observations offers an implicit answer to the third objection to Santayana's ideal of liberation. It is common, as was indicated earlier, for Santayana to be accused of abandoning the Greek ideal of rational harmony only to retreat from life into what he himself termed a 'post-rational' morality — a morality, that is, which turns its back on the world and seeks consolation in some extra-rational faith or vision.

Once again, the criticism contains an element of truth, in so far as Santayana himself did lead an increasingly reclusive life as he grew older. This, however, was a personal idiosyncrasy. The aim of the spiritual life as he presents it in his philosophical writings is not reclusive, but consists simply in a rejection of instrumental attitudes to the world as an ultimate basis for human existence. 'It is the essence of spirit', he wrote, 'to see and love things for their own sake, in their one nature, not for the sake of one another, nor for its own sake' (PSL 93).

Liberation in this sense, then, is not properly described as a retreat from the world. Nor is it properly described as an ideal of self-abnegation or self-mastery. It consists, rather, in a self-possession through which it becomes possible to enjoy 'the pure exercise of those faculties which are truly native and sufficient to the spirit' (PSL 170).

Spiritual liberation in Santayana's sense clearly cannot bring release from the tension between reason and desire which lies at the heart of the human condition. What it brings is reconciliation and affirmation. 'Although spirit belongs intrinsically to another sphere,' Santayana wrote, and therefore 'cannot help wondering at the world, and suffering in it', it nevertheless 'has no unmannerly quarrel with its [material] parents, its hosts, or even its gaolers' (FE 120-121).

What has not yet been considered is the relation between the ideal of spiritual liberation and the political order. This will be examined in the next chapter. For the moment, it will be appropriate to conclude this sketch of the foundations of Santayana's philosophy with a brief indication of its principal strengths and weaknesses.

* * * * * * * *

The main strength of Santayana's naturalism has nothing to do with anything novel it contains. Novelty, indeed, was never his concern: the outline of his mature philosophic system, for example, begins by italicizing the assertion that 'my system is not mine, nor new' (SAF v). Its strength lies rather in its attempt to provide a modern and purely secular language in which to describe fundamental features of the human condition that were well known in the ancient and medieval worlds but have subsequently been obscured by the progressive orthodoxy of the modern age. Three such features in particular are brought back into focus by Santayana's philosophy.

In the first place, Santayana insists that self-consciousness is not self-knowledge. This is the point of his insistence on the need to take the psyche, rather than the individual self as conventionally understood, as the point of departure for ethical thought. The modern concept of the self, Santayana holds, is unsatisfactory because it narrows personality down to reason and will, thereby encouraging a destructive concept of reason as the enjoyment of perfect autonomy. Such a concept of the self permits, above all, the absurd illusion of indeterminacy, which creates in turn a false sense of limitless possibilities. More generally, what Santayana has to say about the madness inherent in human nature reinforces his critique of the modern self.

In the second place, Santayana's materialism provides a means of criticising the rationalist tendency of much western moral and political thought. Abstract ideals — ideals, that is, which are detached from a specific material context — are wholly incompatible with a naturalist philosophy.

Thirdly, his doctrine of essence underpins a sustained onslaught on the instrumentalism of modern culture. In particular, to the almost exclusive emphasis on the primacy of action in the modern world, Santayana opposes an eloquent defence of the contemplative life. If this defence passes unheeded, he observes, we will be left with nothing more than the vague vitalism which is the nearest that modern societies have got to devising a philosophy of life. It is worth pondering on this topic for a moment.

At the popular level, vitalism is no more than the cult of youth, health, and self-assertion. In philosophic terms, however, Santayana found its purest expression in the thought of Henri Bergson, whose work he regarded as a brilliant expression of the most disastrous feature of our age. This is that 'The mind has forgotten its proper function, which is to crown life by quickening it into intelligence, and thinks if it could only prove that it accelerated life, that might perhaps justify its existence; like a philosopher at sea who, to make himself useful, should blow into the sand' (SCW Vol 2, 160). In reality, this vitalism is merely the symptom of a spiritually impoverished imagination, an imagination from which religion has vanished and which is kept stretched on the machinery of business and society, or on small half-borrowed passions which we clothe in a mean rhetoric and dot with vulgar pleasures. Finding this intelligence enslaved, our contemporaries suppose that intelligence is essentially servile; instead of freeing it, they try to elude it. Not free enough themselves morally...they cannot think of rising to a detached contemplation of earthly things, and of life itself and evolution; they revert rather to sensibility, and seek some by-path of instinct or dramatic sympathy in which to wander. Having no stomach for the ultimate, they burrow downwards towards the primitive. But the longing to be primitive is a disease of culture; it is archaism in morals. To be so pre-occupied with vitality is a symptom of anaemia' (SCW Vol 2, 10).

Against the strengths of Santayana's doctrine must be set three notable weaknesses. The first is an underlying didacticism that can occasionally make him more moralistic than the tradition of humanism which is the principal target of his scorn. What is at stake is more than just a mood or tone: it is a spectacular failure of intellectual sympathy. One of the most dramatic illustrations is his essay on 'The Absence of Religion in Shakespeare.'

There Santayana maintains that those, like himself, 'who require a certain totality in our views, and who feel that the most important thing in life is the lesson of it...can hardly find in Shakespeare all that the highest poet could give' (SCW Vol 1 70). The possibility that Shakespeare was not in the business of giving a 'lesson' is dogmatically discounted, and the absurdly patronising conclusion reached that 'Shakespeare himself, had it not been for the time and place in which he lived, when religion and imagination blocked rather than helped each other, would perhaps have allowed more of a cosmic background to appear behind his crowded scenes' (SCW Vol 1 71). In fairness, it should be added that this was the early Santayana, writing before the comic vision came to play an important part in his thought. The didactic tendency to see life in terms of the intellectual lessons to be extracted from it, however, never completely disappeared from his work.

Closely connected with this didacticism is a second weakness, which is Santayana's tendency to rationalisation. The nature and implications of this tendency are well illustrated by a famous essay on the romanticism of Browning, in which Santayana accused the poet of lacking 'the essential conception of any rational philosophy.' His statement of precisely what Browning lacks is the noteworthy point: it is awareness 'that feeling is to be treated as raw material for thought, and that the emotion is to pass into objects which shall contain all its value while losing all its formlessness. This transformation of sense and emotion into objects agreeable to the intellect, into clear ideas and beautiful things, is the natural work of reason' (SCW Vol 1 104-5).

What this passage suggests is that, in spite of Santayana's determined efforts to come to terms with human embodiment, he could do so in the end only by downgrading matter to the status of fodder for spirit. The result is that beauty, for example, becomes a sort of extraneous aura around a material base which it never penetrates. In the case of poetry, as his treatment of both Shakespeare and Browning makes clear, this means that the poetic element is reduced to pleasant packaging for the transmission of thoughts which could have been stated independently of the poetic form, and might possibly have benefitted from being extracted from that guise.

The consequences of this propensity to rationalise are not confined to Santayana's aesthetic theory; they inevitably flow over into his view of human relationships. Passionate love, for example, as his hostility to Browning indicates, meets with stern disapproval, not so much because it is frequently destructive as because it is passionate. Platonic love is preferable, because it is 'favourable rather to abstraction from persons and to admiration of qualities'; but that, of course, is really to say that love is only acceptable in so far as it does not make too many concessions to human nature. Perhaps Santayana is wise, but what is at stake can best be brought out as a third criticism that goes beyond his aesthetic theory and Platonic treatment of love.

The third criticism concerns the very coherence of his naturalism. His aim is to unite spirit and matter in a philosophy which insists upon the dependence of the former upon the latter, while insisting that the sole value of matter lies in its status as the base of spirit. Instead of welding the duality of spirit and matter into a seamless whole, the result is a persistent ambiguity about the nature of their relationship which ultimately leaves Santayana's account of the unity of the self unintelligible.

Finally, Santayana's account of the nature of reason itself suggests that he remained divided between two conflicting tendencies. The main tendency of his philosophy is towards a doctrine of relativism which asserts the inevitable conditionality of all human experience. If he had confined himself to this doctrine his philosophy would have gained considerably in consistency. But Santayana does not seem to have been completely happy about relativism. His doctrine of essences, in particular, indicates a hankering for absolute foundations in philosophy, in spite of his overt rejection of the possibility of finding any. Perhaps this absolutist tendency is partly explained by his Platonic assumption that the eternal and undying is intrinsically superior to the temporal and transitory; but whatever the explanation may be, the outcome is that the duality of spirit and matter noted above — a dualism which Santayana castigates in traditional western philosophy — remains unresolved in his own thought. Despite his harsh words about Kant's dualism, for example, Santayana does not ultimately appear to have got much further.

None of these criticisms, it should be said, would have unduly perturbed Santayana, since formal philosophy is ultimately subordinate to vision. What must now be considered is the relationship between his vision, on the one hand, and his theory of limited politics, on the other.

Chapter 4: Naturalism and Limited Politics

What still remains to be considered are the implications of Santayana's naturalist philosophy for political theory. The most important of these, all the others being indeed merely entailments of it, is Santayana's belief that naturalism enables him to provide the first completely non-ideological theory of limited politics in the history of modern political thought. Such a theory, he considered, provides the only means of rescuing the ideal of limited government from the pernicious illusions with which liberal intellectual orthodoxy has surrounded it during the past two centuries.

This extraordinarily ambitious venture can only be carried through, Santayana maintains, by relocating political science within a philosophy of objective limits. These limits, as the previous chapter indicated, derive from the determinate character of all material existence, including man's own. To work out the full moral and political implications of this materialist theory of limits is the aim of *Dominations and Powers* (1951), Santayana's most notable attempt at the systematic presentation of his ethical philosophy. It is with this work that the present chapter is mainly concerned.

In order to judge the success or otherwise of Santayana's attempt to construct a non-ideological theory of limited politics, it is necessary to examine in some detail the two parts into which his enterprise may naturally be divided. The first consists of an extended critique of liberalism, the purpose of which is to identify the precise nature of the illusions that lead him to reject the liberal-democratic theory of limited government. The second consists of an attempt to sketch out an alternative version of limited government more appropriate to the contemporary world. This takes the form of what a sympathetic critic, John Gray, has aptly termed a theory of 'post-liberal' politics. Although interdependent, the critical and constructive parts of Santayana's political thought will be considered separately for purposes of analysis.

The critique of liberalism

Santayana's critique of liberal-democratic orthodoxy is contained in his identification of five illusions which make it impossible, he believes, for this orthodoxy to provide a coherent account of the nature of true freedom, which he terms 'vital freedom'. This is the freedom of every human being to develop his or her nature in accordance with its specific potentialities.

1. The first illusion: the belief that true freedom is 'vacant liberty'

The whole of modern liberal doctrine, Santayana maintains, has been constructed upon a false assumption about human nature. This is that man is radically indeterminate. Being indeterminate, he may be credited with limitless possibilities. It follows that his good consists in a condition of vacant liberty, since any other kind of liberty would immediately close off some of the limitless possibilities. Belief in the indeterminacy of human nature, in other words, has led liberalism to think of freedom in a way which is inevitably destructive, since any aspect of the social order can be rejected as oppressive, not because it has been tried and found wanting, but merely because it does not correspond to the wholly abstract ideal of vacant liberty. So long as liberalism occurs within a traditional order, Santayana stresses, this destructive potential remains concealed, since the liberal can pose as an heroic reformer, inspired by creative zeal. Once the traditional order has been destroyed, however, it becomes apparent how disastrous the liberal ideal of vacant or indeterminate liberty is in practice. The result may well be a society in which the liberal's emancipated children have no grievances left; but what the liberal did not foresee is that his children will probably also lose their morality,

Naturalism and Limited Politics 79

as well as their grievances. 'Even the abundance of their independent sciences, without an ultimate authority to synchronise or interpret them', Santayana predicts, 'may become a source of bewilderment. Nothing may remain except a mechanical hurly burly, moral disintegration and intellectual chaos' (BR 109).

The liberal concept of the indeterminate self, however, has a further disastrous consequence, which has yet to be noted. If the essential self is indeterminate, then all selves are fundamentally the same, since indeterminate selves are of course indistinguishable. This underlying assumption of the universal sameness of human nature explains the inability of liberalism to come to terms with the most striking feature of human existence, which is the diversity inherent in human nature. It is not difficult, in consequence, to understand the paradox at the heart of liberalism, which is that it claims to defend toleration, but cannot come to terms with human diversity. For reasons which will become still clearer if we now turn to the next illusion, the fate of liberalism is to defend freedom in theory, but to impose a drab uniformity in practice.

2. The second illusion: the belief that the individual is the ultimate social reality

The liberal concept of vacant liberty, Santayana observes, identifies the individual in terms of an impoverished and untenable concept of rationality. Ignoring the material roots of man's life as an animal or embodied being — his existence, that is, as a *psyche*, in Santayana's terminology — the liberal concept of rationality treats man as an autonomous spiritual being, with hopes and aspirations that can be dealt with as if they had no connection at all with the material side of his being.

Having adopted this abstract concept of the individual as a purely rational being for whom embodiment is merely an incidental feature of his existence, liberalism then treats political ideals as if they were disembodied spiritual values to which the inevitable constraints of material life appear as unpalatable obstacles, to be legislated out of existence as quickly as possible. The most disastrous result of this individualism is the doctrinaire egalitarianism which impels liberalism towards the oppressive uniformity mentioned a moment ago.

Now it is perfectly true, Santayana acknowledges, that all men are equal. This is true, however, only in the abstract or purely formal sense that all men are conscious or rational beings. But they are not on that account purely spiritual beings. As embodied beings, or psyches, it is inevitable that 'the quality, scope, and significance of [their] consciousness will differ indefinitely and boundlessly'. It is true that this diversity 'does not in the least nullify the equal appeal of spirit everywhere to brotherly recognition and charity from the spirit'. What must be emphasized, however, is that this appeal 'is only to that mystical insight and disinterestedness of which pure spirit [alone] is capable, when liberated from all special private or earthly attachments.' Recognition of man's abstract spiritual equality therefore establishes no equality 'between persons [*qua psyches*], no unanimity or harmony amongst animal wills' (DP 358). This, however, is precisely what liberalism's high-minded stress on human equality ignores.

In tones of sustained irony, Santayana indicates the unintended outcome of this high-mindedness, which is that the liberal love of abstract equality destroys the respect for natural diversity without which talk of liberty becomes sheer mockery. As the following passage makes clear, the outcome is the conversion of toleration into what he terms the 'euthanasia of differences', ending in 'the peace of moral extinction':

> Open every door, let in the light and air, smile upon the Red Indian in his feathers and the Chinaman in his pigtail, and the diffused and placid twilight of goodwill would bathe the moral universe for ever. Everybody would be happy at home, like the Englishman having his solitary tea in his garden; and all wars would be at an end because, at heart, there would be nothing left to fight for. Good will and mutual acquaintance would gradually rub off those remaining differences. The Chinaman would voluntarily cut off his pigtail; the Red Indian would desire not the white man's scalp but a cloth cap for his own head; and the Englishman

would find it more convenient to take his tea in a teashop, no longer knowing any solitude or any garden. Toleration would have proved the euthanasia of differences. Everybody would be free to be what he liked, and no one would care to be anything but what pleased everybody. Concessions and tolerance and equality would thus have really led to peace, and to peace of the most radical kind, the peace of moral extinction' (DP 449).

3. The third illusion: belief in the political power of 'directive imagination'

The third liberal illusion is what Santayana calls the illusion of 'directive imagination'. Although this illusion is not peculiar to liberalism, but is on the contrary one to which all political activity is inherently prone, a liberal age is more unprotected against it than any other. What then is the nature of the illusion in question?

It consists, Santayana explains, in the belief that human reason has the power to shape history in accordance with whatever ideals the imagination may suggest. What makes liberalism peculiarly prone to this illusion is the same abstract concept of the individual that gave rise to the first illusion. Since the liberal concept of individuality begins by assuming that man is an autonomous spiritual being, with a rational essence quite independent of the material world, it is natural for liberalism to present politics and history as a sphere in which 'little but designs and desires occupy the stage' (DP 8) — a sphere, that is, in which ideas, principles, -isms, and disembodied values contend, rather than flesh and blood creatures who are severely limited by the material world they inhabit.

Directive imagination, Santayana notes, is perhaps the most flattering of all illusions to human egoism, since nothing is so pleasing as seeing things take shape before one's eyes according to one's ideas, no matter what they be (DP 125). This kind of intoxication, he observes, is of course a familiar feature of childhood, when it takes the form of harmless daydreams. Usually, the ordinary course of life subsequently bring with it some compromise with reality. One sphere of life, however, is unique in actually nurturing and feeding upon directive imagination. This is the political sphere. 'The new minister', Santayana writes, 'is again a child...He dreams of speeches applauded, measures passed, elections won...and statues of oneself in public squares' (DP 124). Such dreams are not necessarily mere fantasies: they may well come true. But the important thing is that whether they do or not is entirely a matter of luck, which is precisely what directive imagination fails to appreciate. The defect of directive imagination, in a word, is not that what it envisages is impossible, but that it is unaware of the nature and limits of power. The mistake involved is the same as the one involved in the familiar example of the creature from outer space who concluded that the fly which he saw land on the house was the explanation for the fact that the house happened to fall down a moment later.

So far as politics is concerned, the best example of this inept reasoning is provided by the modern revolutionary. What he fails to understand is that a so-called revolution can only ever *seem* to succeed. Successful revolutionaries, Santayana writes, 'are like malicious doctors at a death bed, who should boast of having killed the patient. They may have wished to do it, and he may have died. They may even have made a fatal injection at the moment when he was about to expire. But he would have died without their help; for if he had been curable they never would have been called to his bedside, nor nursed those hostile intentions. The reformers are themselves symptoms of the public disease' (BR 106).

The modern revolutionary, however, is only the most recent and spectacular manifestation of the power of the illusion of directive imagination. In a more subtle form, this illusion was enshrined at the heart of liberal theory from its first beginnings in the seventeenth century. It took the form of the conviction that the state is the product of consent, along with the concomitant illusion that its value is to be assessed entirely in utilitarian terms. The truth of the matter, however, is that government exists 'solely because it is inevitable' (LR 2,71). It is founded, that is, in human nature, and not in reason or consent. It may of course subsequently become the object of rational approval and consent, but its origin does not lie in them, as liberalism mistakenly believes.

4. The fourth illusion: that self-government automatically means good government.

The fourth illusion crystallizes Santayana's misgivings about modern liberal democracy. It consists in the equation of self-government with good government which has been made in the western world ever since the doctrine of popular sovereignty was propounded in 1789 by the French revolutionaries. The nature of this illusion is the theme of two imaginary dialogues on self-government between Socrates and the Stranger (i.e. Santayana himself) in *Dialogues in Limbo*.

'Our tragedy', the Stranger tells a sympathetic Socrates, 'is an old one, of which you drew the moral long ago; it is the tragedy of those who do as they wish, but do not get what they want. It is the tragedy of self-government' (DL 93). The 'tragic' nature of modern self-government arises from the fact that this is now synonymous — as Socrates notes in amazement — with government by the will of the governed. That, says the Stranger, is 'the foundation of all our politics' (DL 90). Why one must ask, does Santayana consider the liberal-democratic ideal of self-government to be so disastrous?

The answer becomes apparent as soon as Santayana, in the person of the Stranger, explains to Socrates the meaning that is given to the concept of self, in the modern concept of self-government. In his own time, Socrates observes, self-government was thought to be an admirable thing, to be fully achieved only by philosophers, and only with great difficulty and discipline. The modern concept of self-government, the Stranger explains with embarrassment, is completely different. Far from connoting self-discipline, it is wholly uncritical in relation to the flow of human passion and desire, leaving no room for ideal aspiration and the concomitant need for personal discipline. In effect, the modern doctrine of self-government therefore places politics at the mercy of fashion. An incredulous Socrates replies that the Stranger lives in an age which, quite simply, has not learnt how to live, because it does not recognize the need for art, which 'is action guided by knowledge'. Socrates adds that 'without art, the freer a man is the more miserable he must become' (DL 94-95).

At the heart of modern democratic theory, in other words, stands the familiar vacant concept of liberty as freedom to do whatever one wishes, without being subject to any restraints, except those which fashion may for the moment suggest. The democratic ideal of self-government, in consequence, is not really a formula for government at all, but for anarchy. Far from providing the basis for an enlightened and just society, it can only work to destroy what exists, without ever being able to construct a new social order in place of what it pulls down.

This critique of democracy, with its echoes of other patrician liberals like de Tocqueville and Ortega y Gasset, inevitably provokes the charge of gross exaggeration. If liberalism is as destructive a Santayana's analysis suggests, it will be said, how has liberal democracy been able to survive at all? The mere fact that it *has* somehow endured, in a word, seems to convict Santayana of extravagant misrepresentation of the democratic order. Santayana, however, skilfully anticipates this objection.

In practice, he replies, the damage done by liberal orthodoxy has indeed been relatively restricted. But that, he explains, is only because its destructive side has so far been concealed from sight by the survival of a *pre*-liberal moral and intellectual heritage. It is only the persistence of this heritage that has permitted the fundamentally parasitic nature of the liberal dream of emancipation to pass unnoticed. John Stuart Mill, for example, could take for granted the most important feature of the pre-liberal world, which was an ideal of personal discipline and restraint that has in the meantime completely disappeared from modern progressive orthodoxy.

The survival of a pre-liberal heritage, then, has thus far concealed the destructive nature of liberal doctrine. Although something of this heritage still survives, it can no longer counterbalance the destructive dynamic inherent in liberalism, since it has now been reduced to a hollow appendage to industrial and commercial civilization. A good illustration of this situation, Santayana notes, is the survival in the United States of a 'genteel tradition'. The genteel tradition prides itself on preserving old cultural values, but it is a fundamentally arid affair without any creative dimension, floating on the surface of an industrial society with whose daily life it has no organic connection.

In the impotence of the genteel tradition, Santayana saw a symbol of the more general failure of liberalism to provide an adequate foundation for the integration of modern societies. Liberalism identifies the key to integration with culture, but culture, in the liberal interpretation of it, is totally unable to perform the social function assigned to it. Why, it must be asked, does Santayana view liberal faith in culture so sceptically?

The great flaw in the liberal theory of culture, he maintains, is its failure to recognize that 'the flowers of culture... are only proper flowers' when culture itself is firmly rooted in 'the subsoil of uniformity, of tradition, of divine necessity' which is the ultimate basis of human welfare (SCW 2, 23). Liberal theory, however, never acknowledges these roots, since it assumes that culture belongs solely to our spiritual nature. It therefore fails to notice that by destroying tradition, it is in fact destroying the real spring of culture, which is the material psyche. The result is that the liberal view of the world gradually becomes a worthy but emaciated ideology, drifting in an intellectual void. Liberalism is ultimately unable, in consequence, to avoid succumbing to a last illusion which marks its final loss of contact with reality.

5. The fifth illusion: the belief that liberal democratic progress consists in the creation of a society in which power has been eliminated in favour of rule by reason.

The fifth illusion consists in the systematic inability of liberal thinkers to come to terms with power as an integral, and therefore ineliminable, part of existence. Although the inability of liberal political theory to come to terms with power was touched on briefly above, it requires closer attention.

When liberal thinkers do begin to acknowledge the ineliminable character of power (as Foucault did, for example, during the past two decades), they are driven to a false sense of despair. The root of this despair lies in the illusion, prevalent in the west especially since the Enlightenment, that the ideal society is one in which the triumph of reason would automatically mean the complete disappearance of power.

To this utopian tendency of modern western thought, Santayana opposes the vision of existence as a condition from which power is inherently inseparable. Existence, initially at least, means eternal war, for 'Life cannot take or keep any definite form without crowding out, crushing or devouring some other form of life (DP 88). Even love is war — 'war at first against the beloved for favour and possession; ever afterwards against the rest of the world for the beloved's sake (DP 105). Likewise, peace is merely latent war, entailing the disciplining of internal resistance at home in readiness to attack external foes.

A philosophy which identifies power with existence in this way is likely to be suspected today of propagating the cynical doctrine that might is right, and dismissed in consequence as merely a belated echo of the now discredited darwinian vision of the world. For Santayana, however, an ethical philosophy which fails to acknowledge the reality of power will never be able to rise beyond the ideological moralizing to which liberalism is condemned. But it is also true, he fully appreciates, that such a philosophy will remain open to the charge of crude cynicism unless it can clearly distinguish power from domination. How then is this crucial distinction to be made?

The answer, Santayana maintains, can be found by considering two philosophers who placed power in the forefront of their analysis of the human condition, but are frequently dismissed by contemporary liberal theorists as too unorthodox or malign for them to warrant serious attention. One is Nietzsche; the other is Spinoza.

Santayana's admiration for Nietzsche is highly qualified, but on the most fundamental matter of all he believes that Nietzsche was correct: by making power the first principle of all his thought, Nietzsche established ethics on its true foundation (EGP 145). Unfortunately, Santayana immediately adds, Nietzsche was unable ever to distinguish clearly between power and domination. He was unable to do so because he confused a genuine insight with a personal idiosyncrasy.

Nietzsche's insight was that 'all life is the assertion of some sort of power — the power to breathe, for example'. The idiosyncrasy was his extravagant personal admiration for self-assertion, masterful egotism and an ethic of aristocratic heroism; that is to say, for domination (EGP 126-127). The result of this confusion is that Nietzsche unjustifiably restricts the meaning of power to a cult of physical strength. He fails, in consequence, to do justice to the ideal dimension of power, in which it is exemplified in moral strength, rather than in domination over others. It is true that he acknowledges an ideal dimension to power, but he confines this to a romantic cult of vitalism which reduces his proposed transvaluation of values to empty posturing. In a word, Nietzsche's analysis of power remains wholly subjective, being ultimately indistinguishable from an infantile ideal of self-assertion (EGP 128, 134-135).

And yet, Santayana concludes, in spite of all his defects, Nietzsche was on the right path, and it is out of his 'wild intuitions' that the 'man of the future may have to build his philosophy' (EGP 135). In order to advance beyond these wild intuitions, the analysis of power has to be rescued from the purely subjective perspective in which Nietzsche views it. This was the achievement of Spinoza. It is true, Spinoza allows, that existence is a condition of war; but, he adds, this is true only for men who have not reached the level of ethical life. What characterizes this level is the achievement of a disinterested standpoint from which an intelligent sympathy acknowledges the good of others as *they themselves experience it*. The militant assertion of the will, in other words, is now modified by acceptance of the diversity of existence. This regard for diversity is expressed in chivalry, which

Santayana regards as the foundation of civilized life.

Chivalry is the ability to accept moral and social diversity. It presupposes rejection of the basic human yearning for absolute power. To become chivalrous, that is to say, is to recognize without acrimony that other men are entitled to differ from oneself even on matters most fundamental to one. Thus chivalry does not require any abandonment of one's own interests; it does not aim, as liberalism aims, at the elimination of power from the world; what it does is reject man's tendency to attach absolute significance to those interests.

Chivalry is therefore a much harder quality to acquire than the liberal democratic virtue of toleration, since the latter is quite compatible with an egotistical assertion of an absolute claim to superiority. Bertrand Russell, for example, who prided himself on his tolerance, showed a notable lack of chivalry in his inability to accept selfishness and patriotism as natural human characteristics (WD 115-116).

Chivalry, however, is only feasible when it is treated in the context of the more general revaluation of limited politics from a naturalistic standpoint which Santayana believes is necessary. The core of this revaluation is the concept of vital liberty. Unlike the vacant liberty of liberal orthodoxy, which is systematically at odds with the natural order of existence, vital liberty accepts and builds upon that order. It is to Santayana's concept of vital liberty that we must therefore now turn.

Beyond liberalism: vital freedom and the rational society

Before Santayana's critique of liberal-democracy can be weighed, it is clearly necessary to consider what kind of alternative order he proposes. He describes this as a rational society which would be based firmly on the real needs and interests of human beings. In order to construct such an order, we must abandon the indeterminate view of human nature which characterizes liberal-democratic theory and begin by accepting that man is in fact a determinate being. The problem, of course, is to know what human determinacy consists of.

Human nature is not, Santayana emphasises, a static phenomenon, 'immutable or identical in all the members of a particular race or a particular region or epoch,' since the psyche is relatively elastic and vital liberty 'changes its form with the changing phases of life' (DP 59-60). Determinate human nature is not, moreover, something which even the most sophisticated empirical or historical methods of study can define. What we require to know is man's potentialities for realizing vital freedom. These potentialities can only be discerned by an imaginative exploration, of the kind Aristotle conducts, of the tension between the actual and the ideal poles of man's existence. It is from the standpoint of this tension, then, that Santayana proceeds to examine man's relation to the social order in terms of a simple but fundamental distinction between the two kinds of circumstances with which it confronts him. On the one hand, there are circumstances which promote the realization of potentialities. These are referred to by Santayana as Powers. On the other, there are hostile circumstances. These he refers to as Dominations. He adopts both these terms from medieval theology, in which they represented two gradations in the overall hierarchy of angels encountered by the soul in its search for its spiritual good. The principal task of political philosophy as Santayana envisages it in *Dominations and Powers* then, is to distinguish Dominations from Powers, in the light of man's potentialities for realizing vital freedom.

In order to give precision to the analysis of human potentialities, Santayana begins by distinguishing three different kinds of social order in which men may live their lives. He calls them the generative, the militant and the rational orders respectively. The generative order embodies the actual side of human nature, in so far as man is a determinate physical being. The militant and rational orders represent the two different forms which may be assumed by the potential side of human nature. The generative order thus enjoys a primacy over the other two orders, arising from the dependence of the potential upon the actual.

The generative order of society is the one in which all human life begins. All men are members of it by virtue of their material embodiment. It is characterized by primal Will. This is the blind, wholly unreflective urge to exist which is the foundation of all life: the restless, unselfconscious impulse of all living creatures, that is, 'to feed, to grow, to master and possess everything' (DP 44). The generative order, in the end, is a bit like the Hobbesean state of nature. Less misleadingly, however, it may be likened to the jungle. Just as in the jungle, conflict is endemic; but the generative order also resembles the jungle in that conflict is morally blameless, no matter how painful, or even tragic, it may be. It arises solely because the different goods of diverse creatures inevitably make them rivals. In the generative order, finally, natural harmony plays as great a part as natural conflict. This natural harmony is, of course, wholly unplanned and unselfconscious, being the product of instinct, habit and tradition. In the human world, it is characteristically expressed in the form of such non-voluntary institutions as the family and tribe. In particular, Santayana assumes, the best guide we have to what membership of the generative order entails is tradition, and he therefore looks askance at radical change.

In the militant order of society, the unreflective life of instinct and tradition that characterizes the generative order is left behind, being replaced by the self-conscious adoption of ideals which men seek to impose on the flux of nature. When these ideals are in harmony with the generative order they are perfectly acceptable, but what tends to happen is that some particular ideal is elevated by primal Will to a point of absolute value, and any aspect of life which does not fit in with it, or derive from it, is dismissed as devoid of ethical significance. In the militant order, therefore, man easily tends to become like an arrogant spider which refuses to recognize the value or reality of anything that lies beyond the web it has spun out of its own gut. Understood in this way, militancy clearly has nothing to do with criminality, or warlike aggression, or evil: it is, rather, a manifestation of that illusory belief in spiritual autonomy to which Santayana believed every self-conscious creature is unavoidably prone.

Modern political ideologies are excellent illustrations of what is meant by militancy, in the very general sense in which Santayana uses the term. He also regards such religions as Catholicism, Judaism and Islam as instances of militancy. Perhaps the best illustrations of what he means by the term, however, are *Lucifer* and *The Last Puritan*, both of which explore the moralistic essence of militancy. They display in particular, as has been seen, the militant egoism which refuses to find value or significance in anything that has not been constructed, or at least approved, by human reason or will.

This portrayal of the militant order presents a problem which is so important that it must be noticed immediately. It consists of an unresolved ambiguity in the concept of militancy itself. On the one hand, Santayana views militancy naturalistically, in accordance with the overall tendency of his philosophy. In this perspective, militancy is regarded quite neutrally, being no more than a wholly natural feature of all living creatures, in so far as primal Will impels them to assert their distinct identity. From this point of view, it would, of course, be absurd to treat militancy in moral terms, since that would make of it, by implication, a condition in need of a more or less radical remedy.

On the other hand, Santayana frequently wrote as if the militant order is a morally flawed condition, in which man is at least partially tainted by *hubris* or egoism. His outline of the militant order therefore appears to be impaled on the horns of an intractable dilemma: by presenting the militant order in terms of *hubris*, he himself seems to be moving in the moralistic direction which his naturalism castigates; whereas by presenting the militant order in purely naturalistic terms, he makes it extremely difficult to distinguish the militant from the generative order. For present purposes, however, it will be best to pass over the ambiguous nature of militancy and turn to what Santayana considers to be the implications of his distinction between the generative and the militant orders for the purpose of working out an alternative to liberal-democratic political theory.

As has been seen, Santayana believes that the militant order of society is prone to ideological politics. Now the cardinal sin of ideology, he maintains, consists in forgetfulness of the continuity of all human experience with its origins in the generative order. In other words, what militancy tends to forget is that passion, which is the natural and inescapable manifestation of human embodiment, always remains the basis of man's existence. To forget this, however, is to forget that if moral and political idealism is not to prove oppressive — as in the case of the liberal egalitarian doctrines discussed above, for example — then it must be restricted to 'disinfecting' passion, and never transformed into the disastrous quest for a moral and political order in which the passions and all other manifestations of the generative order are treated as irrational survivals of an alien and unacceptable reality.

It will be useful to illustrate briefly the way in which Santayana applies the doctrine of the primacy of the generative order to attack the ideological politics of the militant order. Consider, from this point of view, his critique of the socialist ideal of a perfect community, defined as one from which power has been expelled and in which the only bond is the spontaneous spiritual affinity of the members. The impossibility of the socialist ideal can be brought out, he maintains, by reflecting in particular on the concept of the 'Soviet' developed by Russian communism.

The essence of the Soviet concept is its claim to offer the perfect ideal of a free society. The free society, in this sense, would be an entirely spontaneous society as was just said, with nothing but a purely spiritual bond between men as its foundation. The socialist conception of the individual, Santayana adds, must of course be as pure as the society he is to occupy. This individual must therefore be 'an absolute spirit, grounded in itself and responsible to itself alone', although this absolute spirit is also required, in some way which is never explained, to 'transcend its isolation and feel that exhilaration of living and thinking in unison with a legion of kindred spirits, each no less free and absolute than itself' (OS 187).

Why is it, Santayana asks, that socialist idealism of the Soviet kind inevitably ends by forfeiting its claim to be based on pure spiritual spontaneity, and seeks instead to impose its authority through force, thereby becoming just one more of 'those material dominations and powers amongst which spirit must thread its way'? (OS 188). The answer is simple: the more 'spiritual' man tries to become, the more certain his ruin, since man 'is animal before he is spiritual,... and in his very inventions he merely turns over and ruminates the pabulum which fortune has thrust upon him' (OS 195). Man cannot, that is, break free from his roots in the generative order, as the socialist ideal requires him to do.

Santayana's doctrine of the primacy of the generative order, it may be noticed, echoes (albeit in a different language) Burke's appeal to men to conform to the places assigned them by God within the natural order. For Burke, however, compliance with the natural order merely meant, in practical terms, acceptance of English tradition and, in particular, of the mixed constitution established in 1688. He was able, that is, to reach an amicable compromise with the life and institutions of the militant order. For Santayana, by contrast, intelligent adaptation to man's situation requires something far more ambitious than a Burkean compromise could ever create. This is a rational order which transcends the limitations of the militant order that Burke was able to accept. What must now be considered in more detail is what the rational order involves and how it is to be brought into existence.

In the rational order of existence, men defer only to the authority of things. Human conduct, that is, is determined neither by the blind primal Will which rules the generative order, nor by the equally blind idealism which characterizes the militant order, but by a measured adjustment to the material circumstances of life. Since men are ruled only by things in the rational order, there is no arbitrary domination of man by man, with the result that we come now to the most remarkable feature of the rational order. This is that its members display a universal respect for the diversity of human nature. In this sense, the rational order is the only true liberal society.

In political terms, what rule by the authority of things means is that government must no longer be by prophets, reformers, agitators, politicians, demagogues, or persons elected by majority vote, as at present. Instead, it must be by men 'educated and trained in the science and art of government'. What it requires, more precisely, is 'persons able to discern the possibility...of human ambitions... they should be anthropologists, medical men and scientific psychologists' (DP 434). But how is this rational order to be created?

The rational order, Santayana maintains, cannot be brought about by reason itself, since reason is powerless to direct conduct. Paradoxically, the rational order can therefore only be introduced and maintained by militancy, in the form of action by 'some sworn band of militant enthusiasts in whom the idea of a rational society has become an obsession' (DP 295). Santayana somewhat allays the misgivings about rationalist fanaticism which this may create by emphasizing that the rational society cannot, by its very nature, be created through violent methods. It is obvious, however, that in practice it is most unlikely to be created at all.

It must be emphasized at this point that Santayana is perfectly aware of this practical objection. In fact, he says even if the rational society ever were created, it would not endure for long. It was on this sceptical note that he ended *Dominations and Powers* with a fable in which he imagined the shouts of joy with which its own members would gladly destroy the rational society, not because men are perverse, but merely because human nature is not fundamentally rational. But in that case, why bother with the rational society at all?

Santayana's reply is that practicality is not his concern. The purpose of envisaging the rational society is not to create it, but to provide a means of distinguishing clearly between mere dreams, on the one hand, and genuine human potentialities (even if unrealizable) on the other. In this respect, his method has a long and respectable genealogy beginning with Plato's *Republic*. It is therefore appropriate to pass over the practical difficulties and consider what Santayana thinks would be the four characteristics of a rational society.

The first characteristic is that the rational society would take the form of a universal liberal empire. This characteristic, Santayana believes, follows naturally from the present situation of the world, in which ease of transport and communication means that men are 'positively crying for a universal government, and almost creating it against all national wills' (DP 453). In order for it to succeed, a universal government would of course have to be rational, in the sense of being enlightened and disinterested. This is not, he insists, merely utopian speculation. Even though no empire has yet actually achieved universality or stability, history records several occasions when the world has come in sight of a liberal universal empire (DP 453).

The most instructive instance is Rome, which provides Santayana's model of a liberal empire. Roman history suggests, in particular, that a liberal empire must begin at a purely local level, with the establishment of rational government in a form 'peculiar to an exceptionally gifted and moralized community' (DP 435). He speculated briefly, but inconclusively, about the crucial issue of which nation might be able to offer rational leadership to the modern world. Neither Britain, nor the U.S.S.R., nor the U.S.A., he concluded, was fit to become the successor. The British imperial tradition revealed too much indifference, or even contempt, for subject peoples; forays by the U.S.A. into world affairs displayed a tendency to identify American commercial interests with the good of mankind; and the communist ideology of the U.S.S.R., however noble its concern for the proletariat might seem in theory, had inevitably proved to be a formula for domination in practice, as Santayana's early analysis of the soviet concept had suggested it would.

The second characteristic of a rational society is that its government, whether local or global, 'would be autocratic but not totalitarian' (DP 435). It would, that is, be essentially limited government, in that it 'would speak for the material conditions imposed by nature on the realisation of any ideal without dictating to any person or society what its ideal should be' (DP 435). In practice, limited government of this kind would best be secured by abandoning the territorial and tribal units which continue for the present to be the basis of societies throughout the world and making moral societies the basic element. Membership of these moral societies 'should be voluntary, adopted only by adults with a full sense of their vocation for that special life, and relinquished, without any physical hindrance, as soon as that vocation flagged or gave place to some other honest resolution' (DP 450).

The third characteristic of the rational state, whether local or global, is that it would be extremely interventionist in relation to the economic order. It would be committed, above all, to helping men to achieve security and prosperity, but also to achieving spontaneous satisfaction in work, which is required by vital freedom. There are echoes here, as has often been noticed, of the interventionist liberalism of T. H.

and Bosanquet, with its stress on the state as a hinderer of hindrances. Quite what that would involve, however, Santayana does no more than indicate in bare outline. He foresaw, and approved of, the increasing expansion of the state into the spheres of welfare, nationalised ownership of property and regulation of the economy. Such a state, he considered, 'will probably, and perhaps beneficently, produce rather less than was at first produced by rival capitalists and private enterprise, since there will be less ardour both in running risks and in earning higher wages. Society will be perhaps happier, but more slack and more resignedly traditional. The fever of the nineteenth century for sudden wealth and of the twentieth for mechanical marvels will have yielded to a classic wisdom, at a new industrial level of life' (DP 382). Unfortunately, he did not foresee the possibility that there might be an economic slow-down without any corresponding growth in classic wisdom.

The fourth characteristic of the liberal empire concerns the general nature of the political institutions it would contain. In accordance with the managerial and bureaucratic ethos which inevitably follows from Santayana's advocacy of scientific growth, the executive would be autonomous. The important feature of this executive is not that it should be the legal representative of the popular will, but that it should be morally representative of the nation. Moral representation, Santayana writes, occurs when there is 'an ingrained bent in one person to bring about the existence, welfare, or safety of another' (DP 375). An executive of this morally representative kind might take the institutional form of an hereditary monarchy or a self-perpetuating body like the Roman Senate; the crucial thing is not the precise form of the institution so much as the requirement that it should be 'morally representative of the historic and moral vocation of that nation' (DP 381). The rulers and managers as a whole, Santayana observes, 'would be selected, not by popular elections, but by co-option among the members of each branch of the service, as promotion normally ensues in armies, banking-houses, universities, or ecclesiastical hierarchies' (DP 382). An independent judiciary is desirable, but Santayana believes that its independence exists at the discretion of the executive (DP 423). Parties and elected assemblies may exist, but only when there is such a profound consciousness of unity throughout the nation that they are in fact moral representatives of the people, and not merely politicians who have artificially acquired power.

With this sketch of the rational society before us, it is now possible to confront the central question presented by Santayana's political thought. In a nutshell, this is whether the ideal of 'vital' (or determinate) liberty which he advocates is preferable to the 'vacant' (or indeterminate) liberty for which he castigates the liberal democratic state.

To reply that *in practice* Santayana offers no viable alternative to vacant liberty, is unsatisfactory, for the reason already given. This was that Santayana did not set out with a practical aim in mind: his purpose was always avowedly heuristic. What will be suggested here is that, even within the limits of this purpose, the revision of limited politics which he proposes is deeply unsatisfactory. The reasons why that should be so are perhaps not quite as obvious as they may seem; and to reflect on them is instructive, since it illuminates the theoretical difficulties involved in applying a philosophy of modesty to politics, as Santayana set out to do. Anticipating the gist of what follows, Santayana fails because he himself is ultimately not at all modest about what he expects from politics.

Turning to look at the reasons for his failure in more detail, they may be found in four crucial but implausible assumptions which are either incompatible with limited politics, or else impose a severe strain upon it.

The first assumption concerns Santayana's concept of rational authority. More precisely, it is the assumption that truly legitimate political authority can only be possessed by men who have the status of what he terms 'moral representatives'. Since it is from this standpoint that the parliamentary system of contemporary liberal democratic states is dismissed by Santayana as woefully inadequate, his distinction between legal and moral representation requires closer scrutiny.

The obvious difficulty created by this distinction, regardless of the way in which it is formulated, is that it opens the door to anarchy, by permitting the constitutionally established government to be challenged on the ground that it is not the 'true' representative of the people. There is, however, a deeper, more theoretical difficulty with the concept of moral representation which requires attention.

The difficulty in question emerges as soon as it is noticed that Santayana originally introduced the concept of moral representation in the context of his aesthetic philosophy, to which political considerations were of course irrelevant. It was only at a later stage that he extended it from the aesthetic, first to the moral, and then to the political sphere, without any apparent sense of the problems created by this change of context. This development occurred in the following way.

In his earliest philosophic treatise, *The Sense of Beauty* (1896), Santayana had invoked the Platonic theory of the philosopher in order to defend the objectivity of aesthetic judgments. According to Platonic theory, the philosopher possesses a representative soul, and is therefore able to rise above mere expressions of personal opinions to articulate universally valid judgments. In the aesthetic sphere, where the exercise of coercive power by one man over another is not involved, it is easy to pass lightly over the problem of what happens if disagreement occurs about the philosopher's judgments. In the political context, however, the situation is potentially grave, since the philosopher possesses the power to enforce his own opinion. Plato dealt with the possibility by introducing a Noble Lie which would promote consensus, and hence ensure that the need for coercion never arose. Santayana, however, cannot resort to such a strategy without showing outright contempt for the vital liberty of the population at large. It is not, of course, that Santayana is guilty of duplicity on this matter but rather that the whole issue of coercion is fudged by his unwarranted assumption that consensus may be relied upon to circumvent the problem.

The second assumption which needs to be considered is Santayana's belief that in a rational social order, spiritual or cultural life will be universally accepted as an absolute value. This assumption, however, is quite incompatible with the systematic relativism to which his general philosophic position points. The only explanation for this absolutism, it would seem, is the survival in a modified form of the dogmatic Hellenic idealism which marked *The Life of Reason*, despite Santayana's overt renunciation of moral dogmatism some years after the publication of that work. Whatever the explanation for it, Santayana's absolutism is dramatically evident, for example, at the start of *Dominations and Powers*, when the asserts that: 'In order to obtain anything lovely, I would gladly extirpate all the crawling ugliness in the world' (DP ix). In so far as that is a purely personal credo, it is of course a tenable position to adopt. Unfortunately, it does not remain personal but colours Santayana's theory of government and is therefore at odds with the pluralist regard for diversity which he attributes to the rational society.

The third problematic assumption Santayana makes concerns not so much rational politics as politics in general. It is the assumption, more precisely, that politics can never play a creative role in the construction and maintenance of social harmony. This assumption follows directly from Santayana's claim that the material psyche is the agent in politics. His doctrine of the psyche is valuable as an antidote to the liberal-democratic tendency to assign an exaggerated potency to the will of the supposedly sovereign individual. It has the effect, however, of dismissing *all* politics as the illusory play of directive imagination. The paradoxical result is that Santayana is compelled to deny creative political virtue even to the English, whose political achievements impressed him most.

The great achievement of English liberal democracy, Santayana believes, is to have avoided vacant liberty and maintained a society based on vital freedom. They have done this by instinctively refusing to oppose liberty and discipline. Are they not then to be given credit for this achievement? No, Santayana replies; the English have, in effect, just been lucky. Their good fortune has been to enjoy a pre-political unity which owes nothing to their institutions, but is essentially a natural endowment, rather than a social and political achievement. Thus any attempt to explain the success of English democracy by the practice of majority rule, or indeed by the working of any other English institution, is completely absurd:

> To put things to a vote, and to accept unreservedly the decision of the majority are points essential to the English system; but they would be absurd if fundamental agreement were not presupposed...In a hearty and sound democracy all questions at issue must be minor matters; fundamentals must have been silently agreed upon and taken for granted when the democracy arose...[It follows that] parliaments and elections [i.e. constitutional forms] are never more satisfactory than when a wave of national feeling runs through them [making them superfluous] and there is no longer any minority nor any need of voting. (CO 127-8).

If we look more closely at the pre-political unity with which Santayana believes the English have been blessed, it rapidly proves impossible to say quite what it involves. It is clear that he believes English national unity to be somehow 'natural', in contrast with the 'artificial' unity generated by political propaganda or historical proximity. The difficulty, however, is to distinguish clearly between what is natural and what is artificial. Sometimes he tried to base the distinction on the concept of race, but the meaning of that concept remains ambiguous in his interpretation of it. He attempts initially, for example, to give it a biological meaning, but recognizes that many peoples who are racially distinct manage to co-exist politically. He also acknowledges that the supposedly natural or biological identity conferred by race cannot be clearly distinguished from the artificial identity acquired through shared historical existence. In the course of this existence, he admits, the natural psyche is moulded by the circumstances it encounters and the tradition it acquires. What is left of the original racial identity after contact with history is impossible to determine. For purposes of explaining political unity, it would seem, a naturalistic philosophy appears to be positively misleading.

Finally, the most questionable of all the assumptions which Santayana makes concerns the nature of vacant liberty itself. Since the whole of his critique of liberalism hinges on this, it is important to notice a crucial distinction which gets lost from sight in the course of his sustained onslaught on the ideal of vacant liberty. This is that in its classical seventeenth and eighteenth century form, the essence of liberalism is not a doctrine of *vacant* liberty but of *civil* liberty. Putting the same point in slightly different words, the classical doctrine is not a defence of the indeterminate self, but a critique of arbitrary power. It follows that Santayana's critique of liberal-democracy is based upon a serious misunderstanding, in so far as the original classical ideal of civil liberty continues to play a part in the liberal democratic tradition.

Why does Santayana fail to notice the distinction between vacant and civil liberty? The main reason is that he is concerned throughout his philosophy with the all-pervasive influence of the romantic tradition in the modern world. If *Dominations and Powers* is read as a powerful attack upon romantic politics, then it makes perfect sense; for the very core of romanticism is indeed the concept of the indeterminate self, at which Santayana's sharpest arrows are aimed. Unfortunately, Santayana seems to assume that *all* liberal democratic politics are, almost by definition, romantic politics. In so far as this leaves him indifferent to the survival of the classical ideal of civil liberty, his arrows miss their target and leave him vulnerable to the charge of misrepresentation, and even caricature.

Ironically, the most unfortunate result of Santayana's neglect of the civil ideal is that it would have provided him with a far more satisfactory means of accommodating the diversity which he values than the rational society he envisages. It does that, not by involving the problematic concepts of rational authority and moral representation, but by turning to the formal and procedural ideal of the rule of law. Unfortunately, the formality which makes this ideal a disinterested one tends to be equated with 'vacancy', in the course of Santayana's critique of liberalism.

The main problem, however, is that Santayana expects too much of politics for him to be content with the classical ideal of civil liberty. The liberty he wants is of a far more exalted kind: it is the freedom which comes from reconciliation to necessity and not anything as modest as freedom from arbitrary power. Unfortunately, the grander form of freedom so dominates his thought that the issue of arbitrary power with which classical liberalism is concerned finally disappears from his sight. Its disappearance is apparent when, for example, Santayana writes that 'It is no loss of liberty to subordinate ourselves to a natural liberty' (RS 89). It may indeed be no loss of the vital liberty which comes of rationally acknowledging necessity; but it may quite possibly be the total loss of civil liberty.

It would appear, then, that a politics of modesty must be based on the classical concept of civil liberty, rather than on the grand concept of rational (or vital) liberty. In the latter case, a limited style of politics may perhaps survive, but if it does so, it is only at the discretion of beneficent managers.

Chapter 5: Conclusion

What then are the aspects of Santayana's philosophy most likely to prove of continuing significance? Since his avowed aim was to be neither novel nor idiosyncratic, the answer is not to be found in the discovery of ideas which have never before been placed before the world. His general achievement consists, rather, in reformulating, in purely modern and secular terms, a vision of man whose lineaments may be found in predecessors as diverse as Lucretius, St. Augustine, and Spinoza. The result is a distinctive and eloquent synthesis of age-old ideas which is likely to become more, not less, relevant to the modern age, precisely to the extent that success in the goal of achieving and diffusing prosperity brings a disillusion for which our dominant culture provides no remedy. Santayana recognized that his response to disillusion, which is to embrace it, rather than evade it, would never be a popular one. Nevertheless, it remains suggestive for those who find comfort in lucidity itself.

What is this vision? To end where we began, it is the vision of man as the guest, rather than the master, of a universe with which he may learn to be on tolerable terms, even though it is fundamentally indifferent to his existence. To change man's perspective from that of master to guest is the transvaluation of values which Santayana sought in his philosophy.

This transvaluation is the key to his specific achievement, which was described in the preface as a philosophy of modesty. Since modesty is what the western world has generally lacked, with the notable exception of thinkers like Aristotle, Montaigne, Locke, Hume and (more recently) Oakeshott, Santayana's attempt to explain what it involves is an event of some significance; and the more so, since such a philosophy is likely to prove the only sane foundation for the post-modern world.

Santayana constructs the philosophy of modesty, it will be recalled, without any of the exotic devices usually resorted to by those who have searched for a positive alternative to the predominantly melancholy mood of western modernity: he requires, that is, no Superman, no leap into faith, no inner quest for authenticity, no existential encounter and no mystical search for Being, but only a rigorous scepticism, on the one hand, and a combination of naturalism, humour, piety, courtesy and detachment, on the other.

Santayana's philosophy of modesty, then, is his principal contribution to an age in which the confident anthropocentrism of traditional western culture is no longer tenable. No less relevant, however, is his attempt to apply this philosophy to politics, in order to extricate the theory of limited politics from ideology. By ideology, what is meant in this context is the all-embracing moralization of power which has dominated the western dream of liberation ever since the Enlightenment. To an age which has for long been haunted by an exaggerated sense of human rationality or spirituality, to effect the 'de-moralization' of power by bringing it into contact with the limits imposed on man by his earthly existence, is the first step towards a sane appreciation of the limits of moral and political action.

In this respect, the project which Santayana undertook in *Dominations and Powers* remains the central task of contemporary political thought. Unfortunately, Santayana permitted his attack on the romantic concept of the indeterminate (or 'vacant') self to overshadow all else, with the result that he failed to do justice to the classical ideal of civil society as the form of association most compatible with the diversity he wished to protect. Whether it is in principle possible to reconcile Santayana's neo-Platonic belief in rational authority and rational freedom with the ideal of civil association is a matter which cannot be explored here. It seems inevitable, however, that an irresolvable tension between them would always remain in any conceivable attempt at synthesis. As things stand, Santayana's critique of liberal democracy remains relevant to the extent that contemporary political life in the west has fallen under

Conclusion

the spell of the romantic pattern of thought which he dissects with unerring precision.

It remains, however, to notice briefly some more fundamental weaknesses of Santayana's philosophy. The most important of these arise from the ultimate incoherence of his quest for a naturalistic basis for philosophy. It is not only that the precise nature of spirit and matter, as well as the relationship between them, remains unresolved in his thought. What is no less problematic is his attempt to ground a theory of moral and political limits in a biological version of naturalism which paradoxically echoes the scientism he rejected. If Santayana had abandoned his attempt to found ethics on a wholly objective concept of nature, and had turned instead to a philosophic anthropology based on history, he might have achieved the same end in a more persuasive way. His intention, nevertheless, which was to restore a sense of objective limits to western philosophy, points out the path to be followed.

If the problems posed by Santayana's naturalism are viewed sympathetically, what still remains intact is the criterion by which he always judged the adequacy of every philosophy, from his earliest thought until his death. This criterion is an ideal of balance: balance, not in the sense of a set of truths about man and the world to be weighed against a set of falsehoods, but in the sense of a dynamic balance to be struck between the poles of the various tensions which define the human condition. It follows from such a conception of balance that the task of philosophy will inevitably vary in different ages. In our age, the kind of balance in which Santayana finds the key to a more modest humanism suggests that the emphasis should be placed, as he placed it, on humour, scepticism and materialism.

Finally, what needs to be emphasised once more in order to do Santayana full justice is the ultimately ethical purpose of all his thought. This, he always insisted, is the touchstone by which his work is to be judged. In this perspective, the cogent message behind his philosophy should not be obscured by deficiencies in the concepts he employs. Although this message is as old as the Greeks, it has not been much heeded in the modern world. It is that man is neither a beast nor a God, but lives in a condition of ineliminable tension between the two realms of matter and spirit. To present politics within the framework of this tension, rather than as a possible escape from it, is the aim of his restatement of liberalism.

At a time when religion can no longer offer most men comfort, and when the experience of an indifferent universe is frequently the source of a despair which Santayana himself regards as spurious, a philosophy which prompts sympathy for the jaunty lines of Goethe which Santayana fondly recalled in old age is not to be lightly passed over:

'Iche hab' mein Sach auf Nichts gestellt...
Drum ist's so wohl mir in der Welt' (MHW 6).
(I have built my life on nothing,
Which is why things go so well for me in the world.)

Further Reading

There is a comprehensive bibliography of Santayana's writings down to October 1940, in P. A. Schilpp's *The Philosophy of George Santayana*, Northwestern University, Evanston and Chicago 1940, pp 609-668. There is another, again down to 1940, in Jacques Duron, *La Pensée de George Santayana: Santayana en Amerique*, Librairie Nizet, Paris 1950, pp 529-542. The latter also contains a bibliography of the principal works on Santayana down to 1950.

The best short introduction to Santayana's philosophy is provided by himself, in two essays contained in P. A. Schilpp's anthology (see above). One is his 'A General Confession' (pp 13-30); the other is his 'Apologia Pro Mente Sua' (pp 495-605). The broader vision behind his thought emerges more clearly, however, from *Three Philosophical Poets, Lucifer, The Last Puritan,* and his various volumes of essays. Of the latter, *Soliloquies in England, Obiter Scripta* and *Dialogues in Limbo* are particularly illuminating.

Still at the introductory level, a useful selection from practically all Santayana's writings is contained in Irwin Edman's *The Philosophy of Santayana*, Constable, London 1954. A less comprehensive but very good selection is contained in the two volumes of *Selected Critical Writings of George Santayana*, edited by N. Henfry, C.U.P., 1968. The *Little Essays* drawn from the writings of Santayana down to 1916 by Logan Pearsall Smith with Santayana's collaboration, Constable and Co., London 1920, is also an excellent introductory volume.

So far as Santayana's general philosophy is concerned, a number of critical but sympathetic commentaries are valuable.

Duron, J: *La Pensée de George Santayana* (see above). A thorough study of Santayana's thought down to 1912, when he left America, concentrating in particular on *The Life of Reason* (1905).

Sprigge, T.L.S: *Santayana*, Routledge and Kegan Paul, London and Boston 1974. A very close commentary on Santayana's ontology, epistemology and moral philosophy. Sprigge is only incidentally concerned with Santayana's aesthetic philosophy, however, and not at all with his political philosophy.

Singer, B.J: *The Rational Society: A Critical Study of Santayana's Social Thought*, The Press of Case Western Reserve University, Cleveland/London 1970. A thorough critique of Santayana's political writings.

Singer, Irving: *Santayana's Aesthetics*, Harvard University Press, Cambridge, Mass., 1957. The best study of Santayana's aesthetics.

Wilson, E.C: *Shakespeare, Santayana and the Comic*, University of Alabama Press, Alabama; George Allen and Unwin Ltd., London 1973. This work attempts to do justice to the comic vision as the source of Santayana's affirmative outlook.

Gray, J: 'George Santayana and the Critique of Liberalism', *The World and I,* February 1989, pp 592-607. The best short account of the contemporary relevance of Santayana's political thought, as well as its limitations.

Lieberson, J: 'The Sense of Santayana', *New York Review of Books*, Vol. XXXV, No. 5, March 31st, 1988. At the opposite pole to Gray's sympathetic approach is the comprehensive hostility to Santayana displayed by Lieberson.

Biographical material is provided by Santayana himself in his autobiography, as well as in D. Cory's edition of the *Letters*.

Cory, D: *Santayana: the Later Years*, George Braziller, New York 1963, is particularly illuminating, being the product of close personal acquaintance.

Lind, Bruno: *Vagabond Scholar*, Bridgehead Books, New York 1962, is a lively and evocative, albeit idiosyncratic, account of Santayana at the end of his life.

Butler, R: *The Life and World of George Santayana,* Gateway, Chicago 1960. Mainly interesting for the personal account of Santayana at the time when the author went to see him in 1950, shortly before he died.

Index

alienation   13, 27, 28, 29, 38, 42, 52, 78
America   13, 14, 15, 17, 18, 107
animal faith   62, 63, 65
Aquinas, St Thomas   16
Aristotle   29, 30, 31, 35, 45, 68, 89, 103
Arnold, Matthew   16
Augustine, Saint   103
authority, rational   98, 102, 104
Avila   15, 17

barbarism   23, 38, 39, 40, 41, 42, 47
Beckett, Samuel   9, 38
Bergson, Henri   72
Bhuddism   68
Bosanquet, Bernard   96
Browning, Robert   74
Burke, Edmund   93
Butler, Fr. Richard   20

Catholicism   15, 16, 45, 68, 91
chivalry   87, 88
civil society   104
Christianity   23, 44, 56, 68
Collingwood, R.G.   46
comic vision   50, 51, 52, 53, 73, 108
common sense philosophy   63, 78

democracy   37, 79, 83, 100, 101, 104
Descartes, René   55, 60, 64
directive imagination   81, 82, 99

egotism 32, 38, 40, 43, 45, 46, 47, 87
Eliot, T.S. 14
equality 80, 81
essence 16, 38, 42, 50, 53, 55, 65, 72, 81, 91, 92, 101

Fichte, G. 45
Foucault, Michel 86
Freud, Sigmund 54

generative order 89, 90, 91, 92, 93
Goethe, W. von 39, 40
good government 83
Gray, John 77, 108
Green, T.H. 96

Hamlet 36
heathenism 42, 43, 44, 45, 47
Hegel, G.W.f. 45
Heidegger, Martin 9
Hobbes, Thomas 39, 46
Hume, David 62, 64, 103

idealism 16, 35, 36, 37, 42, 49, 79
imagination 10, 18, 25, 27, 29, 53, 57, 72, 73

James, William 17

Kant, Immanuel 45, 65, 75

Leibniz, Gottfried 45
liberal democracy 83, 84, 100, 104
liberalism 20, 30, 77-86, 88, 96, 101, 102, 106
liberation 55, 66, 67, 69, 70, 71, 104
liberty 78, 80, 84, 88, 89, 97, 99, 100, 102
liberty, civil 101, 102
liberty, vacant 78, 79, 88, 97, 100, 101

Index

Life of Reason 14, 61, 67, 69
life of reason 50, 62
limited politics 11, 75, 77, 88, 97, 104
Locke, John 39, 63, 103
Lucretius 55, 56, 60, 103

madness 31, 59, 72
Marxism 54, 55, 56
materialism 49, 50, 53, 54, 55, 56, 57, 58, 60, 61, 63, 72
militant order 90, 91, 92, 93
Mill, J.S. 84
modesty 5, 21, 53, 56, 97, 102, 103, 104
Montaigne, M. de 11, 103
moralism 16, 17, 24, 29, 30, 31, 32, 36, 47
myth 25, 27, 56, 62

naturalism 20, 47, 49, 50, 57, 61, 62, 71, 74, 77, 91, 104, 105
Nietzsche, F.W. 11, 27, 45, 86, 87

Oakeshott, Michael 103
Ortega y Gasset, J. 84

Pater, Walter 16
piety 32, 33, 34, 35, 37
Plato 24, 29, 30, 52, 56, 61, 63, 64, 65, 94, 98
power 27, 35, 38, 56, 60, 65, 81, 82, 85, 86, 87, 88, 89, 98, 101, 102, 104
Protestantism 44, 45
Proust, Marcel 69
psyche 56, 57, 72, 79, 80, 85, 89, 99, 101

rational order 89, 93, 94
rational society 88, 94, 95, 97, 99, 101
rationalism 24, 34, 35, 36, 47
realism 24, 25, 27, 28, 29, 47
Reformation 24, 44, 45

religion 9, 15, 16, 25, 42, 43, 45, 49, 56, 63, 68, 73
Rousseau, J.-J. 37, 40
Royce, Josiah 17
Ruskin, William 16
Russell, Bertrand 14, 88
Russell, J.F.S., 2nd Earl 14

Sartre, Jean-Paul 9
scepticism 62, 63, 64, 66
self 33, 37, 50, 54, 55, 56, 57, 58, 67, 69, 72, 75, 79, 104
self-government 83, 84
Shakespeare, William 73, 74, 108
Socrates 12, 24, 28, 31, 64, 83, 84
soul 30, 37, 44, 55, 66
Spain 13, 15
Spinoza, Benedict 7, 10, 55, 86, 87, 103
spirit 18, 31, 33, 35, 36, 39, 43, 46, 49, 50, 56, 57, 58, 60, 65, 70, 71, 74, 75, 80, 92, 93, 105
spiritual life 57, 68, 70
Swinburne, Algernon 16

The Last Puritan 19, 35, 38, 42
Tocqueville, Alexis de 84
tragic vision 53
transvaluation of values 11, 87, 103

United States 14

vitalism 72, 87

Weber, Max 9